SIGHTINGS

DISCOVERING GOD'S PRESENCE IN OUR
EVERY DAY MOMENTS

LYNN AUSTIN

LYNN AUSTIN BOOKS

Dear Reader,

One of the most amazing and comforting promises that Jesus gives us is this: *"And surely I am with you always, to the very end of the age"* (Matthew 28:20). But in the busyness of our daily lives, in the challenges and surprises we often face, we don't always have a sense of Christ's nearness. We forget to notice all of the little messages He sends to remind us that He is right beside us, watching over us, weaving all things together into a glorious tapestry for our good and for His glory.

Instead of leaving God behind after our Sunday morning worship or our daily devotions, what if we tried to cultivate that sense of His presence in our ordinary moments? What if we watched for Him at home and at work, and everywhere we went? This book is a product of my attempt to do just that. It's a collection of my thoughts and ponderings as I've learned to look for "God sightings" in the simple moments of my life. I'm learning to see patterns of His redemption everywhere! And to see myself as He sees me—precious and worthy of His love.

I hope you can learn from this book, so that you, too, will begin to notice all of the times and places where Jesus shows up in your everyday life. Because the truth that we can cling to, no matter what our days may bring, is that we are always in God's hand.

Blessings,

Lynn

WEEK ONE

"Lord, You have assigned me my portion and my cup; You have made my lot secure. The boundary lines have fallen for me in pleasant places; surely I have a delightful inheritance." Psalm 16:5-6

ONE

PLAYING, WRITING... AND PLAYING

"For we are God's workmanship, created in Christ Jesus to do good works, which God prepared in advance for us to do." Ephesians 2:10

I HAVE A CONFESSION TO MAKE. While I grew up in a household of readers—my mother was the town librarian—I was never a reader as a child. And I couldn't sit still long enough to write!

I loved books when someone else read them to me. My sister Bonnie used to "read" to me when she was 5 and I was 3. I also loved listening to my mother read bedtime classics like *Uncle Wiggly* and *Charlotte's Web*. My grandmother was a natural-born storyteller who could keep me spell-bound for hours on warm summer evenings with tales from her childhood. But I didn't want to read or write in my spare time, I wanted to play, living out all the wild stories in my imagination.

I had neither the time nor the patience to sit still with a

book when I could be a character from *Treasure Island* or from a story I created. I lived in the world of my imagination like the little boy in the cartoon *Calvin and Hobbes.* That stuffed tiger was real, even if no one else could see it. My bicycle was a real horse and I galloped down the street with the wind in my face, my pigtails flying.

I CREATED elaborate stories for my sisters and friends with plots and storylines that lasted for days. We were cowboys and Indians. We were pioneers who made great, epic journeys in our Red-Flyer "Conestoga" wagons packed with our baby dolls and food supplies. The fields and woods near our house were vast, uncharted wildernesses where we might encounter pirates or find buried treasure. We camped out in makeshift tents in our backyard during the summer, imagining that we were great explorers on safari. The dark, creepy cellar of our 100-year-old house became the setting for many spine-tingling mysteries.

THE ONLY WRITING I did besides school assignments was a play entitled *My Old Kentucky Home.* We performed it in our backyard and charged the neighborhood kids 5-cents each to watch—my first writing income. I barely remember the plot but as the production's security chief, it was my job to protect our backyard theater from spies until the performance.

I took my job very seriously and decided to stage a drill to keep everyone on their toes, making up an outrageous story about seeing a man in a yellow shirt skulking around. Unfortunately, my story was so convincing that it caused panic in our neighborhood as rumors of a mysterious stranger spread. How could I explain to all the concerned adults that there was a huge difference in my mind between telling a lie and using my imagination? One thing was clear, my early fiction was very convincing.

I DIDN'T DISCOVER that I enjoyed writing until I was in my thirties—and then it was like coming home, returning to my childhood, living in my imagination all over again. I loved it! Once again, I could live all sorts of adventures by putting myself in my characters' shoes, making up stories, creating new worlds. Researching my historical novels is one of my favorite parts of this writing life. I love visiting the places where my characters lived, seeing what they saw and smelled and touched. By "playing" in all of these places, my imagination is set free to create.

When I'm writing, I live in my imagination like I did as a child, creating stories that will take my readers to faraway places and times. Writing is play for me—and of course, it's also very hard work! But the adults don't yell at me any more for telling lies. Now I get paid to do it. Best of all, I get to share my faith, incorporating the lessons God is teaching me into the lives of my characters. I wouldn't trade my life for any other!

WE'RE NOT ALL CALLED to write books. But I do believe that God has created each of us with unique gifts and talents that we can use for His glory. When we discover what they are, and joyfully use them, we honor Him and are blessed in return. As Mother Teresa said, *"Not all of us can do great things. But we can do small things with great love."* If we invest our talent and serve Him with joy, we will hear our Master say one day, *"Well done, good and faithful servant! ... Come and share your Master's happiness."*

Prayer

Heavenly Father, help us to listen to our hearts and to Your still, small voice so we can discover the purpose for which You created us. Help us to find the work You created us to do, for that is our highest calling. Give us joy in our labors, knowing that when we serve one another with love, we are serving You.

TWO
NEVER GIVE UP

"We also rejoice in our sufferings, because we know that suffering produces perseverance; and perseverance, character; and character, hope." Romans 5:3

ASPIRING writers often ask what my number one piece of writing advice is. My reply? Never give up! I know that sounds obvious, but becoming a writer can be a long and difficult path, a roller coaster ride filled with challenges and discouragement. I know, because I nearly gave up before I ever got published.

I began writing more than twenty-five years ago when I was a stay-at-home mom, living in Canada with my husband and three children. After a great deal of work, I completed my first novel, *Gods and Kings*, and began the long, tedious process of sending my book proposal to publishers, getting rejected, sending it out again, and trying not to get discouraged. Then one glorious day I finally heard back from a Christian publisher in the U.S. who said, "We like your proposal—please send us your complete manuscript for review."

This seemed like great news, but after nearly a year went by, I was still waiting. At last they told me that the manuscript had one final hurdle to clear before they would decide whether or not to offer me a contract.

This was the era before cell phones, so I hung around my house for two anxious weeks, fearful of missing the phone call that would change my life and set me on the path to realizing my dream. But instead of the telephone, my doorbell rang one day. It was my mailman, delivering a black plastic garbage bag with my name and address taped to it. My first thought was, "Don't I have enough garbage? Someone is mailing me more?" But when I opened the bag, there was my manuscript!

The pages were in complete disarray, tossed haphazardly into the trash bag as if someone had turned on a fan and thrown the pile in the air. Several pages had footprints on them. Others had tire tracks. This had to be a mistake. I rooted through the bag and found the box I had used to mail the manuscript, battered beyond recognition. It must have burst open somewhere between the U.S. and Canada, and the post office had kindly shoveled the mess into a garbage bag to deliver it the rest of the way.

I sifted through the disheveled pages and finally found the letter from the publisher. It said, "We're sorry, but we've decided not to publish your book." The trash bag seemed like a prophetic sign to me. Not only had my book been rejected, it was garbage. I gave up writing.

I HAD WORKED as a teacher before my kids were born, and since my youngest was now ready for kindergarten, I decided to sign a teaching contract for the coming school year. But God has His ways of turning us around when we're heading in the wrong direction, and a few months into my new job, I began to feel like Jonah in the belly of the whale. I was under so much stress at work that I became ill three different times during that school year with three different stress-related medical conditions. After I found myself flat on my back for the third time, I surrendered and asked God to show me what He wanted me to do. His answer—write!

And I was immediately successful? Not even close! I did resign from teaching, but a few more years passed before *Gods and Kings* was finally published. It became the first novel in a five-book series that has been translated into several languages. I get letters from readers all over the world telling me how much the book has blessed and inspired them.

WHAT IF I had given up for good? I can't answer that question, but I do know that the suffering I endured when I walked away from God's calling, drew me closer to Him in the end. And maybe that's why our dreams aren't always instantly fulfilled. Maybe God delays them so that we will learn to call on Him and to trust Him. So, my advice to anyone who is pursuing their dream will always be "never give up." Continue to persevere, even if your dream comes to your door in a garbage bag.

Prayer

Heavenly Father, we want instant results, and You want a relationship with us. You want us to learn to hear Your voice and to trust Your perfect timing. Help us to use our times of waiting, and disappointment, and frustration to draw closer to You.

THREE
WHAT ARE YOU WAITING FOR?

"Yet the Lord longs to be gracious to you; He rises to show you compassion. For the Lord is a God of justice. Blessed are all who wait for Him." Isaiah 30:18

DO any of us enjoy waiting? In shopping lines? In traffic? At the doctor's office? Or for our prayers to be answered? This morning, the psalm I read during my quiet time said, *"Each morning I bring my requests to You and wait expectantly"* (Psalm 5:3). While it's true that I wait expectantly for God to answer my prayers, I don't always wait patiently.

AT THE MOMENT, I'm waiting for several urgent prayers to be answered. A job opportunity for a loved one. My friends' six-month-old granddaughter who needs a liver transplant. A friend's husband who is battling cancer. For a friend awaiting a biopsy report. These are only a few of many. And don't we all have similar lists?

Right now, winter has a solid grip on the area where I live. The Lake Michigan beach where my husband and I walk looks cold and desolate, locked in a deep freeze, waiting for renewed life. If I had no memory of the countless spring-times and summer-times that have followed winter in the past, I would sink into despair to imagine the world forever looking this way. But I do remember, and remembering gives me hope.

HOPE ALSO COMES in the form of the prayer journal I keep so I can look back on the many prayers that God has answered in the past. Last year alone, a dear friend had successful back surgery. A young father I'd been praying for finally began an addiction program. My long-awaited grand-daughter was born healthy and strong. Celebrating each of these answers gives me faith as I wait for God to answer the others. Slowly but surely, I'm learning to wait.

I WAITED eleven years from the time I first began to write fiction until my first novel was published. When my prayers were finally answered and I received my first book contract, I rejoiced. But during the long publishing process for that first book, my editor and I had a disagreement that brought me to my knees. Could I accept the changes she wanted to make, or would I have to cancel the contract and find a different publisher? I prayed while I waited for the publisher to respond to my concerns. I waited. Then I waited some more.

When my patience ran out, I picked up the telephone, intending to give someone a piece of my mind and end the agonizing wait. Seconds before dialing my editor, I happened to glance at my computer. The screen-saver was programmed to display random Bible verses, and this one read, *"Wait for the Lord; be strong and take heart and wait for the Lord"* (Psalm 27:14.)

I laughed and put down the phone. And waited some more. In the end, the disagreement was resolved to everyone's satisfaction. My books were in print.

I STILL DON'T LIKE WAITING but I think I'm growing better at it. Like the psalmist, *"Each morning, I bring my requests to God and wait expectantly."* And hopefully. So, what are you waiting for?

Prayer

Thank you, Lord, for always hearing our prayers.
As I wait for your answers, help me to remember that You are a faithful, loving God. You always know the best way and the perfect time to answer each one.

FOUR

ARTHUR'S STORY

---

*"This is how we know what love is: Jesus Christ laid
down His life for us. And we ought to lay down our lives
for our brothers."* 1 John 3:16

I WAS AN EAGER, conscientious student in elementary
school. I wanted straight A's. I wanted the approval of my
teachers. My 6th grade teacher, Mr. S, was one of my favorites.
Energetic and creative, stern yet fair, he was generous with his
encouragement and affirmation. If students did something
noteworthy, Mr. S would honor them by writing their name on
the chalkboard in huge letters, where it would remain for the
rest of the day. I loved seeing my name up there.

In our small, rural community, everyone knew their class-
mates and their families. We were similar in many ways. Then
one day, a new student joined Mr. S's class who was noticeably
different from the rest of us. Arthur was the only student in the
entire school with black skin. His clothes and shoes were more

tattered than ours. He stood a head taller than the other boys and was probably older, but he had been placed in 6th grade because he could barely read.

His family had come to our fruit-growing area as migrant workers, and he spoke with an accent that was probably Haitian or something similar. It was hard to tell, because Arthur barely spoke. No one befriended him.

ONE DAY IN CLASS, the topic of foreign languages happened to come up, and Mr. S asked if any of us knew words from another language. Hands waved in the air. Students recited words they knew. Mr. S turned it into a contest and began keeping score. My hand waved wildly. I knew quite a few German words that my grandmother had taught me. I could even recite a little rhyming prayer in German.

I started counting my collection of words on my fingers as I awaited my turn and knew I was certain to win. But first, it was Arthur's turn. He raised his hand for the very first time and told us he spoke French. All eyes were on Arthur. Mr. S gushed with enthusiasm as Arthur spoke phrase after phrase. I kept score and still believed I might be able to beat him with my German poem.

MR. S APPLAUDED when Arthur finished. His name went up on the chalkboard in huge letters. Arthur beamed as if lit from within and gave us his very first smile. Then Mr. S moved on to another subject. But wait! I didn't get my turn! Didn't Mr. S see my hand? I battled tears. It wasn't fair.

I WAS TOO immature at the time to see the wisdom and grace

in Mr. S's actions. But in later years I understood, and the lesson has remained with me to this day. It was something Jesus would have done. In describing the coming Messiah, the prophet Isaiah writes, *"A bruised reed he will not break, and a smoldering wick he will not snuff out"* (42:3).

IN A CULTURE THAT SAYS, "ME FIRST" and demands my rights above all, I want to be more like Jesus, who *"made Himself nothing, taking the very nature of a servant"* (Philippians 2:7).

Prayer

Lord Jesus, I pray that You will help me to see the bruised reeds all around me and to love them as You do. Give me a heart of compassion to tend and nurture these bruised ones the way You would, regardless of the cost to me.

FIVE
THE GIFT

"Do not neglect your gift" 1 Timothy 4:14

IT WAS ALMOST CHRISTMAS, when a woman who enjoys reading my books said to me: "God has given you a wonderful gift." Maybe it was the season of the year, but I immediately pictured a beautifully wrapped present.

A gift! I did nothing to earn it or deserve it. Unlike Santa Claus, God doesn't give gifts to "nice" children, and lumps of coal to "naughty" ones. My delight in telling stories and any ability I have to do it well, came to me as a free, no-strings-attached gift from a loving Father who chose it especially for me. I'm not a member of some select group who was chosen to receive a gift while others were excluded.

WHEN EXPLAINING GOD'S GIFTS, scripture says God *"gives them to each one, just as He determines"* (1 Corinthians

12:11). No one is left off His list. And He has a huge variety of gifts to give besides the ability to write books.

Our family always gives each other presents at Christmas. I love thinking of each individual person on my list and choosing something special for each one. I enjoy seeing my loved ones' pleased reactions when they open them, and I especially enjoy seeing them use the gifts I've given.

I hope they will think of me each time they do, the same way that I remember the people who've given me certain cherished gifts over the years. I would be so disappointed if the people I love kept their gifts wrapped up beneath the tree, unopened and unused.

HERE'S THE THING—I know many, many people who aren't even aware that God has given a gift to each of us, the most important one being the gift of His Son, Jesus Christ. Sadly, their gifts remain unopened instead of being used and enjoyed. I've also met people who acknowledge that they may have been given a gift such as writing ability, but they choose to wait for the perfect set of circumstances to open and use it. "When I have more time," they say. "When the kids are grown." "After I retire." Too often, that perfect time never comes.

I was the mother of a nine-year-old, a two-year-old and a newborn when I first sat down and started to write. If I had waited for ideal conditions, I would still be waiting! I took an important step in unwrapping my gift when I signed up to attend a Christian writers' conference. That's why I love to say "Yes!" whenever I'm now asked to teach at a conference.

I ESPECIALLY LOVE WATCHING little children open their presents, don't you? I love seeing their anticipation and enthusiasm, their sheer joy as they tear off the wrapping paper and pull out something special. Why not be like a child and tear into the gift that your loving Heavenly Father has delighted in giving you? Please don't wait another day!

Prayer

Thank You, Heavenly Father, for creating each one of us so uniquely. Please give us the courage and faith to see ourselves as You see us, so we can unwrap the special gifts You've given us and use them for Your glory.

Something More...

"Now about spiritual gifts, brothers and sisters, I do not want you to be ignorant . . . He gives them to each one, just as He determines." (1 Corinthians 12: 1, 11)

It took me years to recognize that God had given me a gift to write books, even though teachers and friends often encouraged me to write. Why couldn't I believe that something I was good at doing, something I enjoyed doing, was exactly what God created me to do?

My biggest hurdle was fear. Fear of failure. Fear of making a fool of myself. Fear that I was wasting my time. Those fears caused me to make excuses for not pursuing my gift. But as my faith grew, God helped me to conquer my fear.

Have you taken a close look at the gift God has given you? Scripture assures us that He has given each of us at least one gift. It's usually something we're good at and enjoy doing, which is why we often overlook it, not recognizing it as something special. Write down some of the things you're good at doing, things that come naturally to you. Are there things that others have said you are especially good at doing?

Or maybe you're making excuses, like I did: "I don't have time . . . I don't have the ability . . . I don't know where to begin . . . I'm too afraid." Make a list of all your excuses:

Now ask God to show you how to begin crossing off each one. For example, if fear of failure is one, pray for courage and faith to do the impossible. Remember, *"I can do everything through Christ who gives me strength"* (Philippians 4:13).

Do you know what your God-given gift is? If you aren't sure, or if you haven't unwrapped it or used it for His glory, why not ask Him now, in prayer?

Prayer

Lord, open my eyes so I can truly see the unique gift You have given me. Give me the courage to work with You, hand-in-hand, to develop it, and use it for Your kingdom.

WEEK TWO

"But You, O God, are a compassionate and gracious God, slow to anger and abounding in love and faithfulness." Psalm 86:15

SIX

A CHILD IS BORN

"How great is the love the Father has lavished on us, that we should be called children of God! And that is what we are!" 1 John 3:1

OUR OLDEST SON, Joshua, was born in Bogota, Colombia where we lived for two years while my husband performed in Colombia's National Symphony Orchestra. Those were interesting and memorable years—learning a new language and adjusting to a different culture far from home. When our friends and family learned that I was expecting our first baby, they invariably said, "But you're coming home to the States to give birth, aren't you?" I just laughed and assured them that babies were born in Bogota every day. It was no big deal. **Until I went into labor.**

. . .

THOSE OF YOU who have children can probably imagine that giving birth is not something you want to attempt to do in a foreign language. Especially when it's your first child. But I was young and dumb—and by the time the labor pains started it was much too late to book a flight to America. I did my best to stumble through the ordeal in Spanish, and when they finally laid little Joshua in my arms, my first words to him came out in Spanish. My baffled husband said, "What are you doing? He speaks English!"

Twenty days later, it was Christmas Eve. We were far from home, far from family, with a tiny son who barely weighed 6 pounds, celebrating the holiday alone. Yet I will always remember it as one of the most beautiful, memorable ones of my life.

CHRISTMAS IN BOGOTA is celebrated like our Fourth of July—with fireworks. You can forget about "Silent Night" with explosions of all kinds going off in the streets. At night the sky is lit up with *globos*, which are little parachutes fastened to cans of burning fuel. They look lovely as they rise up in the sky, but beware—when the fuel runs out, the cans drop to the ground, falling on unsuspecting pedestrians' heads!

BUT WHAT MADE that Christmas so memorable was that I was holding and nurturing a tiny, helpless baby—a beautiful reminder of how tiny and helpless Jesus was when He came to earth. Imagine! The Creator of the infinite universe was once as helpless and vulnerable as my son. From the moment I first held Joshua in my arms, I felt such a fierce love for him, stronger than any emotion I had ever known—and in that moment I finally caught a glimpse of God's unfathomable love for me. For me! I knew that I would protect my son with every last ounce of strength I possessed. Yet God's love for me was so great that He allowed His Son to suffer and die. For me.

That Christmas in Bogota was different from any other Christmas, before or since. We didn't have a Christmas tree. There were no decorations, no lights, no frantic shopping trips. No carols, no cookies, no presents to wrap, no family gatherings. Yet in that simplicity, I found the true meaning of Christmas—a helpless child, a Father's love.

I WAS REMINDED of Mary and all that she must have endured that first Christmas—a long journey from home, searching for a place to stay, giving birth for the first time. Then all of the excitement as the shepherds paid a visit and spread the news about the Messiah's birth. Yet in the midst of it, *"Mary treasured up all these things and pondered them in her heart."* In the simplicity of my first Christmas with a newborn, I had the luxury of doing the same.

EVERY YEAR AT CHRISTMAS, I pray that I can let go of all the trappings, all the stress and hassle for just a few moments, and remember how it felt to hold a helpless child in my arms, a child I loved with all that I am. Like Mary, I want to treasure up these things and ponder them in my heart. And then I can celebrate Christmas joyfully, thanking a Heavenly Father who loved me enough to give His Son for me.

What if, not only at Christmas, but during all of our stressful, busy days, we set aside a few moments to ponder in our hearts the unfathomable love of God? I think it might bring everything else in our lives into a much clearer perspective.

Prayer

Lord, help me to slow down today so I can treasure the wonder of Your love for me. Thank you for giving us Your precious Son so that we can become Your children. May Your gift and Your love inspire me to love You more, and to love others as myself.

SEVEN
FINISHING WELL

"I consider my life worth nothing to me, if only I may finish the race and complete the task the Lord Jesus has given me—the task of testifying to the gospel of God's grace." Acts 20:24

I'VE BEEN CONTEMPLATING ENDINGS, lately, as I near the conclusion of my current work-in-progress. After 330 manuscript pages and more than 100,000 words, the end is in sight. I'm still not exactly sure how the book will end, since I'm one of those crazy writers who makes up the story as I go along, rather than plotting it ahead of time. I figure if I can't guess what's going to happen (and I'm two-thirds of the way through writing it), then readers will be kept guessing, too. I hate predictable endings!

. . .

THERE ARE some important things that I do need to consider in order to finish well. Some of the essentials of a good ending that I've discovered over the years are:

1. The pace should be picking up, with the highest levels of emotion and drama.
2. There should be a sense of closure where I deliver on the "promise" that has kept reader engaged.
3. The end should bring a resolution and a release of built-up tension—the bomb is defused, the murderer discovered.
4. There should be a sense of accomplishment in the main characters' lives. Even if some of their problems remain, the central conflict is resolved and the characters come away changed.

ALL OF THIS must happen as the story reaches a climax. Author Anne Lamott explains the climax as, "that major event...that brings all the tunes you have been playing so far into one major chord." As I lead up to that climax, I'll re-read my novel to look for all of those "tunes" so I can decide what that major chord should be. I'm not quite there yet, but I'm getting close. I want to finish well.

AT THE SAME time that I'm working on the big build-up to "The End," all of nature outside my office windows is doing the same thing. Everywhere I look, the trees and bushes are building up to a grand finale in dazzling technicolor before winter brings the end of another year. And from the look of things, nature is finishing very well.

THERE IS another ending that I don't like to contemplate very often, and that's my own end. A month from now, I'll be another year older. It's not one of those big decade birthdays but I'm getting close. It occurred to me that I'm also about 2/3 of the way through my life. Scary thought! And like my novel—and nature—I want to finish well.

All of my life, I've been making up my story as I've gone along. There have been plenty of surprises, a lot of drama, a lot of emotion. And just like writing a novel, there are a few things I want to consider before I reach "The End."

1. The pace should be picking up. I want to be like the hero in my novel *Fly Away* who decided to live every day of his life to the fullest. He wanted to "die living."
2. I pray that my life will have a sense of closure. That I will have used my talents and gifts well in serving God, fully investing them as His faithful servant.
3. I don't want to leave any relationships in my life unresolved. I hope to live each day asking others for forgiveness, and extending forgiveness to them.
4. There will probably never come a time when every issue in my life is perfectly resolved, but I hope I can look back and see how God has been shaping me, using my struggles to make me more like Christ.

AS I REFLECT on my life, I'm starting to see how all of the "tunes" God has given me have worked together to form a beautiful chord. Even those discordant melodies that seemed so unpleasant to me at the time, have worked together to accomplish God's plan. And I'm looking forward to learning some new songs in the years ahead, too.

Prayer

Lord Jesus, Your death brought eternal life to me and glory to Our Father. You alone know when the end of my days will be. Until then, please give me strength and wisdom to live each day according to Your will, so I can hear You say, "Well done."

EIGHT

HIDDEN TREASURE

"So God created man in His own image, in the image of God He created him; male and female He created them." Genesis 1:27

TWO OF MY favorite hobbies when I'm not writing are bicycling and hiking in the woods with my husband. Now we've added something new to these adventures—geocaching.

It's a treasure hunt, of sorts. Avid fans of this sport hide thousands (if not millions!) of "caches" all around the world in out-of-the way places, then give GPS coordinates and clever hints for how to find them. We searched for some while vacationing in Florida, when visiting our son in California, and when we traveled to Germany. I found a few while hiking in New York State with my sister. They are everywhere!

. . .

A GEOCACHING APP on our phones locates them using GPS coordinates. The compass then takes us within a few feet of where it's hidden. After that, we use the hints that are provided and our powers of observation to find the hidden container. Some are hidden right along the trail. Others require bush-whacking through underbrush or reaching into holes—not my favorite things to do.

Large caches are the size of a shoebox. Medium ones the size of a sandwich container. Small ones, a medicine bottle. Micro caches are even tinier. I'm pretty good at the larger ones. The micro-sized ones often defeat me. Some caches offer little trinkets inside as a reward. I found a dollar bill in one. All of them have some sort of log book to sign. But for me, the reward is in the pleasure of the hunt and the thrill of discovery.

RECENTLY, I've been trying to apply my new treasure-hunting skills to my spiritual walk. Our pastor has been preaching about the *Imago Dei*—the image of God—which resides in every person on earth. The Bible says we were made in God's image, so that spark is hidden there, whether we see it in someone or not. The key to loving our neighbor as Jesus taught, is to remember that even the most unlovable people are made in His image, although we may need to search hard to find it.

Sometimes I meet strangers and feel an instant connection —and discover that they have a huge cache of faith and love of Christ in their hearts. Their treasures are easy to find. Then there are people who rub me the wrong way, or whose outward behavior is offensive, or who don't seem to have any redeeming qualities at all.

Those are the ones I want to turn away from and give up on without even bothering to search. It seems as difficult as finding a micro-cache in a forest. But unlovable people have been made in God's image too, and deserve to be shown His love. Weren't we all "lost" at one time?

JESUS WAS amazing at finding that spark of the divine image in unlikely people such as tax collectors, prostitutes, and demoniacs. And I'm supposed to become more and more like Him, aren't I? He taught us to *"love your enemies, pray for those who persecute you,"* but I never quite understood how to do it. Maybe the key is to search for that hidden treasure of God's image.

Jesus also tells us why we should bother to look: *"that you may be sons of your Father in heaven. He causes the sun to rise on the evil and the good, and sends rain on the righteous and unrighteous."* He doesn't want anyone to remain lost—and so I shouldn't, either.

I OFTEN WISH I had a handy app to make it easier, but I do have the Word of God to guide me. If I'm faithful to follow it, that should be more than enough.

Prayer

Lord Jesus, sometimes it's so hard to see difficult people the way You do, and even harder to love them as You do. Help me to remember that we are all made in Your image, and that Your love is available to every one of us. Teach me to love the way You do.

NINE
WELCOME HOME

"Let all who take refuge in You be glad; let them ever sing for joy. Spread your protection over them, that those who love Your name may rejoice in You." Psalm 5:11

DEXTER IS A RESCUED CAT. He was found wandering in the streets of Chicago and was brought to the Red Door Animal Shelter where my daughter, Maya, sometimes volunteers as a foster parent for stray cats. We call her the "Cat Whisperer" for her ability to calm and tame strays like Dexter —and he needed a lot of taming.

Big, boisterous and street-smart, Dexter didn't get along with the other cats and went stir-crazy in the crowded confines of the shelter. Maya agreed to foster him until he settled down and a permanent family could adopt him. She brought him home to meet her sleek, tawny Siamese, Leonidas.

. . .

I ADMIT I didn't like Dexter, at first. He was too rambunctious and seemed to bully our much-smaller "grand-cat." But as the months passed and Maya worked her magic through love and discipline, I grew to appreciate Dexter's unique personality. He liked to sleep in strange places, like the bathroom sink. Or on my son-in-law's bass guitar. Or on top of my bookshelf when he came to visit. He once found a place to sleep on my fireplace mantel. And at Christmas, he slept beneath my tree, as if hoping he might go home as someone's Christmas present.

Maya taught Dexter how to sit on command. How to play fetch with his little plastic ball. And how to play kitty-cat video games on her I-Pad. He loved those games, chasing birds or catching fish, and quickly reached level 3.

AND THEN ONE day the animal shelter called. They had found a permanent home and a family for Dexter. It happened so fast that I didn't get to say goodbye. When Maya called to tell me the news that he was gone, I felt a hole open up inside.

I realized how much I would miss him, how much I had grown to love that large, rambunctious ball of shedding, white fur. We were happy for Dexter, sad for ourselves.

Leonidas missed him, too. They had become friends. Leonidas wandered through the empty rooms as if searching for Dexter, meowing plaintively. Maya felt so bad for him, she wondered if she should foster another cat. I didn't think I could take the heartache a second time.

A WEEK later the shelter called. Dexter was back! His new owners were unhappy and so was he. Would Maya consider taking him again? I think we all wept with joy. She told me, "If a cat can smile, then Dexter was grinning from ear-to-ear when he walked into our house."

She and her husband adopted him. Dexter now belongs to them. He has a home at last as part of our family.

I THINK the reason that Dexter's story is so heart-warming is because it's our story. In Christ, we were rescued from our former life, redeemed and made new, then adopted into the family of God. I don't ever want to forget what my life would be like without Christ. And I don't ever want to take my rescue and adoption for granted.

But what about all the people around us who are still lost and wandering? In gratitude for what Christ has done for me, shouldn't I do what I can to rescue the lost and help them find a home in Him, too?

Prayer

Lord Jesus, thank You for paying the price to rescue me when I was lost and unlovable. All that I have and all that I am today are because of Your great love for me. Please give me Your love for the lost and broken people around me. Help me show them Your love.

TEN
ON STAGE

"Always be prepared to give an answer to everyone who asks you to give the reason for the hope that you have."
    1 Peter 3:15

LAST APRIL, when we were in California visiting our son Benjamin, my husband and I asked him to get tickets to watch a TV show being filmed. He was able to get seats at Universal Studios to watch the taping of two episodes of "Family Feud" with host Steve Harvey. We sat in the second row, front and center, and had a ball!

The young man doing the warm-up act got the audience all fired up with his antics and contests. That was a terrific show all by itself. Then Steve Harvey came out and he had us laughing until our sides ached. A lot more goes on during the taping than ever ends up on the show—and that man is funny!

He remained on stage during the commercial breaks and treated us to a comedy routine. He also answered questions from the audience that had been submitted earlier. We weren't treated like a living "laugh-track" but as an audience that he was eager to entertain.

DURING THE FINAL COMMERCIAL BREAK, Steve asked us to stay seated after the taping ended because he wanted to send us away with a word of encouragement. We did, and he walked out to the edge of the stage and gave us his testimony of how God had worked in his life. He told his own story, from his heart, and said, "This is what God did in my life, and He can do the same for you. God loves you. He wants a relationship with you."

We were people of all ages, races, and backgrounds, yet no one uttered a sound as we listened. He had won our respect with his humor, his genuine warmth, and his honesty during the show, and now we listened. "You know there's a God," he said with a smile. "You know there is. He's reaching out to you because He loves you."

Steve Harvey entertained me that afternoon, and then he taught me something. He showed me how powerful it can be to simply tell others what God has done in my life. I don't need to memorize verses or have a theology degree, but simply tell my story and remind people that God loves them. I was also amazed that a man of his stature in the entertainment world was courageous enough to use the platform God had given him to speak so forthrightly.

NOT ONLY DID the audience hear his testimony, but the cameramen, technicians, producers and stagehands did, too—

people Steve works with every day. I was reminded that God gives each of us an "audience" to reach out to, whether at work or at school, at home or in the marketplace. He made me wonder—am I taking advantage of the places God takes me and the people He puts in my path to bring Him glory? Do I take time to offer a word of encouragement like Steve Harvey did? Hats off to you, Steve Harvey, for a great show and a memorable lesson.

Prayer

Lord God, You have given each of us new life through Your Son, Jesus Christ. We should be willing to spread that Good News to everyone we meet—and yet we sometimes hesitate. Give us the courage and boldness today to simply tell someone who doesn't know You, what You have done for us.

Something More...

"You will receive power when the Holy Spirit comes on you; and you will be My witnesses...to the ends of the earth." (Acts 1:8)

Can you remember a situation where you shared your faith with a non-believer? How about a situation where you could have testified, but you didn't? Some of us, like Steve Harvey, find it very easy to share our faith. While others, like myself, become shy and tongue-tied.

A few years ago, I attended a seminar where I learned some tips about testifying to non-believers. The leader asked us to write down our story in three parts: what our life was like before Christ; how we met Him; and how our life has changed because of Him. Some of us had very dramatic stories. Most of us didn't. No one's problems were solved instantly, but the changes that Christ brought were very real: peace, joy, purpose, a sense of His nearness and love. And hope.

Take a few minutes to try this exercise yourself:

Before I met Christ, I

Then, I met Christ when

Now, my life has changed

. . .

Once we put our story into words, it becomes much easier to recall and retell it whenever a situation arises. We meet people every day who are searching for peace and joy and hope. People who feel lost and unloved. We don't need to recite a host of Bible verses or debate theology with them. All we need to do is share our story of how Christ came into our life and changed us.

In the courtroom, a "witness" simply tells what she has seen and heard and experienced. Why not take a few minutes to write down your story so you'll be ready to share it with others who need Christ?

Prayer

Lord, thank You for loving me and changing my life. Please help me to put my testimony into words so that I will be ready and willing to boldly share with others what You have so graciously done for me.

WEEK THREE

"Your love, O Lord, reaches to the heavens, You're faithfulness to the skies. Your righteousness is like the mighty mountains, Your justice like the great deep."
Psalm 36:5

ELEVEN
WRESTLING MATCH

"Therefore, my dear brothers and sisters, stand firm. Let nothing move you. Always give yourselves fully to the work of the Lord, because you know that your labor in the Lord is not in vain." 1 Corinthians 15:58

HAVE you ever prayed about a decision but when you followed through on where God was leading, everything went wrong? You probably asked, "Did I really hear from God? How could He allow this to happen?"

MY NOVEL, *Waves of Mercy* tells the true story of the Dutch immigrants who settled the town of Holland, Michigan in 1846. These faithful Christian men and women who had suffered religious persecution in the Netherlands, prayed about what to do and felt God leading them to America, where religious freedom was guaranteed. So, they left beautiful, centuries-old cities to move to the virgin wilderness of Michigan and live in crude log cabins. That first summer, malaria struck the community killing many settlers.

A year later, a ship called the *Phoenix*, carrying 225 passengers, including 175 Dutch immigrants, caught fire and sank in Lake Michigan, five miles from their destination. 180 men, women and children died. As the bewildered immigrants buried their loved ones, they must have asked, "Did we really hear from God? How could He allow these tragedies to happen?"

I BATTLED similar questions when writing my first novel, *Gods and Kings*. I had an opportunity to go to Israel on an archeological dig to research my book, and it seemed like an answer from God. To earn money for my trip, I babysat for three small children along with my own three kids. My husband encouraged me to go and volunteered to take over while I was away.

A few days before I was supposed to leave, our three children came down with chicken pox. Then we discovered that my husband had never had chicken pox, and he became extremely ill. I called the tour organizers to try to cancel or at least postpone my trip only to learn that it wasn't refundable, nor could I re-book my flight.

I would lose all of the money I had worked so hard to save. In spite of his illness, my husband still encouraged me to go— while someone from church called to say, "I think it's clear that God wants you to stay home and be a wife and mother, not a writer."

HAD I really heard from God about being a writer? Why had

my family become sick at the worst possible time? I wrestled with God for answers.

It's in these times of wrestling that we often find ourselves drawing closer to God. I think of Jacob who returned to the Promised Land with his family at God's command. Yet before he reached home, he learned that his brother, who had once threatened to kill him, was coming with a large army of men. Jacob wrestled with God all night long, and was changed from Jacob the "deceiver," to Israel, which means "he struggles with God."

AS I WRESTLED with God about my trip to Israel, the reading for my morning devotions happened to be Psalm 48: *"Walk about Jerusalem, go around her, count her towers, consider well her ramparts, view her citadels, that you may tell of them to the next generation . . ."* I decided to trust God to take care of my family, and walked into my calling as a writer. The novel I researched, *Gods and Kings*, has since been translated into nine languages.

AND WHAT HAPPENED to the Dutch settlers in my novel *Waves of Mercy*? I won't reveal any "spoilers" in case you haven't read the book, but if you visit the town of Holland, Michigan today, you'll find that the immigrants' faith remains strong and vibrant. The town, with a population of 33,000, has more than 71 churches, including Pillar Church, built by the first settlers in 1856.

Prayer

Heavenly Father, we can become so discouraged, at times, that we begin to question whether we have truly heard Your voice. Speak to us, Lord, and give us the faith to persevere through those difficult times, knowing that You have a plan and a purpose for each of our lives that goes beyond what we can see.

TWELVE
TIME TO PULL WEEDS

"This is to my Father's glory, that you bear much fruit,
showing yourselves to be my disciples." John 15:8

I KNOW there are people who love to garden. They enjoy nurturing seeds, planting bulbs, and planning perennial beds so that gorgeous flowers flourish in every season. My neighbor is one of them. I walk past her home and sigh with envy at her creativity and diligence.

I AM NOT one of those people. While I do love the end result when my garden looks pristine and welcoming, I don't enjoy doing the work to make it so. Nevertheless, I was forced to become the family gardener when my husband pulled a muscle in his shoulder. The weeds had no pity on his injury and quickly staged a take-over.

Can anyone explain to me why weeds are so hearty and

fast-growing while their beautiful, cultivated cousins need pampering? Or why the deer and the rabbits ignore the weeds and munch on my plants as if they're a salad bar?

AS I TACKLED our overgrown garden, it occurred to me that the process has some similarities to the way I write. My first drafts are usually an overgrown tangle of words. My strategy is to conquer the blank page and get something down, no matter how bad it is, and then go back and fix it later. It takes away some of the anxiety if I don't stop to critique my work as I write.

The day eventually comes when I have to weed out the overgrown mess. Finding weeds in the garden is usually simple: if the roots seem to go down to China, it's probably a weed. If it pulls out easily—oops! That was probably something expensive.

When I make my first editing pass on my manuscript, it's easy to find the weeds, especially if I remind myself of the rules of good writing.

I ENDED up with a large recycling bin full of weeds by the time I finished pulling them, but the garden still looked over-grown. I needed to go back with my shears and trim away some of the good bushes and plants, too. I hate doing that because I'm always afraid I'm going to cut too much and kill the plant.

It's the same with my manuscript. Even after the weeds of poor grammar have been pulled, my beautiful prose sometimes needs to be trimmed. If I'm in an especially critical mood, I can come dangerously close to chopping away too much and ruining it. Nevertheless, it has to be done.

· · ·

IT WAS VERY GRATIFYING to stand back and look at the results of my gardening efforts. And while I hated to sacrifice writing time for the task, when I finally sat down to write again, I was able to tackle some much-needed editing with renewed fervor.

NOW WHAT ABOUT weeding my spiritual garden? Jesus said, *"I am the vine; you are the branches"* and *"my Father is the gardener. He cuts off every branch in me that bears no fruit, while every branch that does bear fruit, he prunes so that it will be even more fruitful."* That sounds a lot like gardening and editing, doesn't it?

God is looking for fruit like love, joy, and patience—and not weeds like anger, gossip, and bitterness. If I hope to look like my neighbor's garden in Jesus' eyes, I think I have some work to do.

Prayer

Lord Jesus, I know You want my life to be fruitful. Please help me to see the weeds that are hindering my growth and to get rid of them. Help me not to fear Your season of pruning, but to remember that it's for my good and Your glory.

THIRTEEN
THE SABBATH TABLE

"Remember the Sabbath day by keeping it holy. Six days you shall labor and do all your work, but the seventh day is a Sabbath to the Lord your God. Exodus 20:8,9

ONE OF MY favorite weekend pastimes is celebrating the Sabbath with our Jewish family and friends. In the hours before I arrive, they will have been hard at work baking bread and preparing enough food to last for the next 24 hours. The table is beautifully set, and the aromas that waft from the kitchen make my stomach rumble.

I sit down to enjoy the long, leisurely meal with a huge sigh of relief, knowing that a full day of rest lies ahead of me, one in which I don't have to race around multi-tasking or accomplishing everything on my to-do lists. All of the preparations have been completed.

. . .

THE HOST BEGINS the meal by saying a blessing over the bread. There are always two loaves as a reminder that when the Israelites wandered in the wilderness with Moses, God provided twice as much manna on the eve of the Sabbath so the people could enjoy a day of rest. Our host breaks the bread into pieces and passes it around to everyone at the table.

NEXT HE SAYS the blessing over the wine, which is also passed around. The rituals of bread and wine remind me of communion and Christ's command to *"Do this in remembrance of me."* I can easily picture Jesus' disciples remembering His words and His sacrifice every Sabbath as they repeated this tradition.

ONE OF THE Ten Commandments says to *"Remember the Sabbath day to keep it holy,"* meaning it should be different and set apart from ordinary days. The Sabbath food is special and often costly. We dress in our nicest clothes.

There is singing and laughter and joy as we take our time eating and enjoying our family members and friends. Or to use an old-fashioned word, "communing" with them. I usually don't want the Sabbath meal to end.

LAST SUNDAY we celebrated Communion at our church. I arrived frazzled and overwhelmed after a terrible week. I felt wounded and defeated. Then our pastor repeated Christ's words over the bread and wine, and invited the congregation to come to "Christ's table." This traditional invitation struck me in a brand-new way.

I heard Christ inviting me to His table—a Sabbath table.

He had completed all the work. The bread and wine had been bought with a great price. Now He invited me to come and to enjoy a time of close fellowship with Him.

I heard His words as an invitation to rest, and more importantly, to rest in Him. I could stop struggling and striving. I was His beloved. I didn't have to do any work to earn His favor except to believe and accept His invitation.

MY PICTURE of the Sabbath table merged with the Communion table. I now think I understand Christ's invitation in Matthew 11:28 a little better: *"Come to me, all you who are weary and burdened, and I will give you rest."* It's an invitation well worth accepting.

Prayer

Lord Jesus, I thank You and praise You for dying on the cross in my place. I know I could never do enough or be good enough to earn God's forgiveness. Whenever I'm tempted to try, help me to remember that I can find rest in You.

FOURTEEN
THE SECRET

"As a bridegroom rejoices over his bride, so will your God rejoice over you." Isaiah 62:5

THE FAIRY-TALE-THEMED WEDDING WAS LOVELY. My husband's nephew and his bride made a beautiful couple. Afterwards at the reception, the DJ invited the bride and groom and all the other married couples out onto the dance floor for a Generations Dance.

It was crowded at first, but each time the DJ called out an anniversary—five years, ten years, and so on—couples who had been married for only that length of time had to sit down. At last, only the bride and groom and the longest-married couple remained.

I WAS SURPRISED to find that Ken and I had won. We've

been married for more than 46 years. The DJ handed us a microphone and asked us to tell the new bride and groom the secret of our long, happy marriage. I'm not sure how I replied, having no time to prepare.

I'VE THOUGHT about it a lot since then and here are two of our "secrets."

- The most important one is to build your marriage on the foundation of Christ. Since a Christian's life-goal is to love and serve and glorify God, marriage becomes very difficult when your partner has a conflicting goal.
- What's more, a successful marriage is going to require grace and forgiveness many times over, and this doesn't come naturally to us. We learn what true love and forgiveness really are from God, who continues to love us in spite of our stupid mistakes, and who forgives us at great cost. The secret of a happy marriage is to follow His example and love each other sacrificially.

Ken and I were fresh out of college when we married, and we each had dreams and goals for our lives. The first goal for Ken was a graduate degree at Yale University, so I postponed my dreams for a few years and worked to support us. His bigger dream was to play full-time in a symphony orchestra, and so after graduation when he won a position as principal trumpet in the National Symphony Orchestra in Bogota, Colombia, we left family and friends to move to South America.

We did the same thing a few years later when Ken won

principal trumpet in the orchestra in Thunder Bay, Ontario and later in Winnipeg, Manitoba for a total of eleven years of Canadian winters.

IN THE MEANTIME, our family was growing, and my first dream was to be a stay-at-home mom to our children. Ken took several jobs in addition to the orchestra so I wouldn't have to work outside the home: teaching, music minister at a church, and even playing in a dance band until the wee hours of the morning. When I began to pursue my dream of writing, Ken immediately became my greatest advocate and cheerleader.

I'LL NEVER FORGET the day he brought home our first computer—an expense we couldn't afford. I hadn't published a single word, but he told me he believed I would become a great writer, someday. And so, my second secret to a long and happy marriage is to take time to prayerfully plan and dream together. Then do everything you can, and sacrifice whenever you can, to help your partner fulfill those dreams.

THE COVENANT GOD makes with us in Christ has similarities to the one we make in marriage. Jesus drew us to Himself in love. He promised to never leave us or forsake us. His love for us is self-sacrificing, always forgiving and nurturing. He desires only the best for us. In the Book of Revelation, we are pictured as the Bride of Christ, and we will one day celebrate the marriage supper of the Lamb with Him. A wedding feast! In the meantime, my prayer is to become more and more like Christ in the way that I love others.

Prayer

Loving Lord, our sin nature makes us naturally selfish. We can only love others well when we recall Your self-sacrificing love for us. Help us to grow and change and become more like You in the way we live and love.

FIFTEEN

DIFFERENT

"Blessed are the peacemakers, for they will be called sons of God." Matthew 5:9

THE YOUNG MAN who stood alone on the pier, gazing out at Lake Michigan was different from me in many ways—his age, his ethnicity, and his style of clothing, to name a few. But like me, he obviously had come to the beach on this warm, fall afternoon to enjoy the gorgeous day and picturesque view. Because I'm a shy, quiet person, it never occurred to me to speak with him. But my girlfriend Cathy is naturally friendly, and she struck up a conversation with him. I decided to step out of my comfort zone and join in.

EARLIER THAT MORNING IN CHURCH, our pastor had encouraged us to stop looking at the things that divide us—our political views, our economic status, our religion, our gender, sexual orientation, race and ethnicity—and learn to see the *Imago Dei*, the image of God, in the people around us.

After a political season that left our country fractured and angry, the pastor challenged us to be peacemakers, bringing shalom and "wholeness" to our little corner of the world, one person at a time.

And so, in spite of my discomfort, I began talking with "Jason." I quickly learned that he didn't fit any of the stereotypes that I had assumed from his outward appearance. In a warm, soft-spoken voice, "Jason" told us that he was new in town and hadn't made many friends, yet.

He had moved here from a huge city because he wanted a different life from the one he'd been living, and a new start. He now had a good job as a restaurant manager, and a nice apartment. And he loved coming here to the beach to watch the ever-changing lake.

We enjoyed a pleasant conversation and warm laughter then went our separate ways. I would like to think that as we spoke, any stereotypes he may have had of me were shattered, as well. Because as different as Jason and I are, we're also the same in the most important way of all—beloved by God.

I PRAY that from now on, I'll approach people differently. Talking with Jason gave me a tiny taste of how wonderful it is to see people as individuals, not in categories. It makes me wonder how many other "Jasons" are all around me who I've unfairly characterized as "different."

And while I don't plan on making it a habit to strike up conversations with strangers on the beach, I do plan to look at how much alike the people around me are instead of noticing our differences.

. . .

I WANT TO BE A PEACEMAKER, bringing shalom and wholeness wherever I go, one person, one conversation at a time. Imagine how the world could be healed if each of us did the same?

Prayer

Heavenly Father, forgive me for judging others by their outward appearance without knowing what's in their heart. Help me to remember that we have all been created in Your image, and to seek out and kindle that spark of the Imago Dei in each person I meet.

Something More...

"You are the light of the world. A city on a hill cannot be hidden...let your light shine before men, that they may see your good deeds and praise your Father in heaven." (Matthew 5:14-16)

One of the traits that helps me as a writer, is that I'm content to be alone, with only my imaginary characters to "talk" to. Even when I take a break to run errands, my thoughts are often on my novel, making me oblivious to people around me. When it comes to reflecting God's love, my solitary nature becomes a hindrance.

I once read a quote that challenged me to do a better job of loving others: *"You might be the only Bible that your neighbor will ever read."* If the Holy Spirit is alive in me, shouldn't it be obvious to the people I meet? Here are some thoughts that have helped me do a better job.

1. Remember to smile. Joy is one of the fruits of the Holy Spirit, and is something that few unbelievers have. It should show on my face.
2. Practice patience—another fruit of the Spirit— especially when people make mistakes or I'm forced to wait. God is patient with me!
3. Do a random act of kindness—another fruit. In fact, search for someone who could use a little help.
4. No matter how frustrated I am, practice self-

control. "To err is human—to forgive is Divine" and I want to be like Jesus.

5. Give someone a compliment or word of encouragement. Gentleness is a very rare fruit of the Spirit.

6. That leaves peace and faithfulness (see Galatians 5:22).

Can you list a few ways to demonstrate those two fruits of the Spirit?

Which of these might you put into practice today?

Can you brainstorm a few more ideas that will help you shine brightly for God's glory?

WEEK FOUR

"You, O Lord, keep my lamp burning; my God turns my darkness into light. With Your help I can advance against a troop with my God I can scale a wall."
Psalm 18:28-29

SIXTEEN
DAD AND CHARLIE

"I tell you the truth, he is happier about that one lost sheep than about the ninety-nine that did not wander off. In the same way your Father in heaven is not willing that any of these little ones should be lost."
    Matthew 18:13-14

MY HUSBAND KEN had a best friend growing up named Charlie. In a time when kids rode bicycles all over town, explored down by the creek, and played outside until the stars came out, Ken and Charlie did it all together. They were in the same Cub Scout troop, attended the same elementary school, built model cars together. When Ken's dad took him fishing and on overnight camping trips in the woods, Charlie came, too. Those trips became even more meaningful after Charlie's dad died at a young age.

The best friends lost touch after they graduated from high

school and went to different colleges. But when Ken attended his high school reunion this year—his first ever—there was Charlie, also attending his first reunion. It's amazing how much these two men still have in common, and how they've bonded again as if the years had never passed. Then Charlie told us a story that touched my heart.

When he was fourteen, Charlie gave his life to Christ. His youth leader told him to think of a special person who didn't know the Lord, and make a commitment to pray for him every single day. Charlie chose Ken's dad.

DAD WAS A KIND, gentle man who worked as a master woodcarver for an upscale furniture company most of his life. His parents divorced when he was young, and being poor, he didn't fit in or feel welcome among church-going people. He left school after the eighth grade and went to work to help support his mother and sister. Even after he married and had six children of his own—my husband being the youngest—Dad never felt comfortable enough or "good" enough to attend church.

He was a wonderful, loving father in every way, which is why his family and adopted family members like Charlie, loved him so much. But he never said a word about faith in God.

IT'S SO hard to find a way to talk to our closest family members about our faith and our need for Christ. We get together every year at holidays like Christmas, and we want so badly to lead our loved ones to Jesus—and we just can't seem to find a way or the words to do it. And so, the years pass and we always hope there will be a better time, an easier way to say what's on our heart. And much too often, the end comes before we ever have a chance.

Charlie faithfully prayed for Dad every single day—all through his college years, all through the years that he and his wife were raising their family. He moved to a different city, and he and Ken weren't in touch any more, but he continued to pray, wondering if his prayers had ever been answered.

Before he died at age 82, Dad went into the hospital for the last time. Charlie's mother happened to work in the same hospital, and remembering him from their days as neighbors, went up to his room to see him. She asked how he was doing, and Dad said, "I'm at peace. I've given my life to Jesus, and I'm at peace." Charlie's prayers had been answered at last.

CHARLIE'S STORY challenges me to do two things. First, to never, ever, stop praying for family members to give their lives to Christ, no matter how long it takes. I'm praying that I'll find the right opportunity and the right words to say, and to do so in a loving way. Second, I'm challenged to make a commitment, like Charlie did, to faithfully pray for someone who has touched my life, even if I may never know if or when those prayers are answered.

BUT I DO KNOW that we'll see Dad in heaven, someday. And for that assurance, I say, "Thank you, Jesus." And thank you Charlie.

Prayer

Lord Jesus, I hold before You my precious loved one who still doesn't know You as Lord and Savior. You are the Good Shepherd who never stops searching for Your lost sheep. Grant me the right words, at the right time, to share Your love and help bring them home to You.

SEVENTEEN
OPEN TO THE SKY

"The Lord will keep you from all harm—He will watch over your life; the Lord will watch over your coming and going both now and forevermore." Psalm 121:7

ONE OF MY favorite things about celebrating the Feast of Sukkot with our Jewish friends and family members is building and decorating a Sukkah or booth on our back deck. First, we construct a frame out of two-by-fours then enclose three of the sides using tarps. Next comes the fun part—decorating it with natural materials such as cornstalks, cat-tails, and pine boughs. We had cuttings of mint and Russian sage from our garden this year, which made the inside smell wonderful!

Last come the homey touches—adding a tablecloth and napkins, candles, hanging lanterns, even pictures. This year the weather cooperated and we were able to eat all our meals in this outdoor booth without getting rained on or bundling up in countless sweaters.

. . .

THE JEWISH PEOPLE live in booths to remember how God watched over them and protected them and provided all their needs while they wandered in the wilderness for forty years. And so, one of the "rules" for creating an authentic sukkah is that the roof cannot be totally enclosed. You're supposed to be able to see the sky and the stars overhead when you look up, and remember that God is watching over you. He's got you covered.

THE FEAST of Sukkot (sometimes called the Feast of Tabernacles) is one of the three yearly feasts that the Jewish people were commanded by God to celebrate. It comes at the end of the agricultural year and, like our Thanksgiving Day, celebrates the harvest.

We know from the Gospel of John chapter 7 that Jesus obeyed the commandment and went up to Jerusalem to celebrate the feast with His disciples.

I FIND it interesting that God made celebrating Sukkot a commandment. That's how important He thought it was that His people take time to stop and remember everything He has done for us. To remember how He has provided everything we need—including a bountiful harvest.

In the description of the feast in Leviticus God says several times to cease working! This is a day of rest! You shall do no work! It's an act of trust. We can stop working—He has us covered.

. . .

AS THE FEAST of Sukkot approached this year, I was already behind on writing my latest novel. I couldn't afford to stop working for the holiday. Besides, I'm no longer bound by the Old Testament Law, am I? Yet I really wanted to spend time with my family and friends!

In my daily devotions, I happened to be reading the book Rhythms of Rest: Finding the Spirit of Sabbath in a Busy World by Shelly Miller. She teaches that one of the reasons we stop work and rest as God commanded is as an act of trust.

We need to remind ourselves that the world won't stop spinning if we take a day of rest from our work. God has everything under control. In other words, instead of looking frantically around at all the things we need to do, we need to look up!

THERE IS no limit to His ability to supply all of our needs if we simply trust and obey—the way the Israelites did when they lived in tents in the wilderness. I can rest and trust. So, I turned off my computer for five days while our family was here, and I celebrated this feast of joy. And guess what? When I added up my page count at the end of the month, I had completed even more pages than the quota I had assigned myself.

I WONDER what would happen if I lived each day of the year this way? If, instead of trying to keep all of my many plates spinning like a circus juggler, I remembered that God commands me to rest for my own good. He offers rest as a precious gift.

I can almost imagine Jesus sitting in a sukkah with His disciples, looking up at the open sky and saying, *"Consider the ravens: They do not sow or reap, they have no storeroom or barn;*

yet God feeds them. And how much more valuable you are than birds!"

Prayer

Heavenly Father, You rested from Your work on the seventh day and gave us, by example, a day of rest. You formed us and know our need for rest even if we foolishly ignore it. Forgive us for refusing this gift and for continuing to labor as if our priorities are more important than Yours. Thank you for commanding us to rest.

EIGHTEEN
THIN AIR

"You will receive power when the Holy Spirit comes on you; and you will be My witnesses in Jerusalem, and in all Judea and Samaria, and to the ends of the earth."
Acts 1:8

MY HUSBAND and I went for a week's vacation in Rocky Mountain National Park in Colorado, and what a wonderful time we had! First of all, we were surrounded by God's beautiful creation everywhere we looked—magnificent mountains, rushing streams, abundant wildlife. It was so easy to praise God every waking moment and remember His awesome majesty and power.

Second, I got to do one of my favorite activities every day—hiking in the woods. The scenery was refreshingly different from the familiar forests and beaches here in Michigan where I walk every day. There were mountains everywhere I looked!

. . .

BEST OF ALL, we were able to spend time with one of our sons, our daughter, our son-in-law, and our grand baby on this vacation. We shared a family cabin together and were able to relax and talk and eat and hike every day.

I HAD BEEN hard at work on a book before this vacation, and I admit I was feeling a little stuck. My brain felt like it was filled with molasses, and the words and ideas just weren't coming. I needed a break and a change of scene. Maybe some new inspiration. Thankfully, I got all of those things—and something more.

ON OUR FIRST day of hiking, I found myself huffing and puffing after about five minutes of walking. I thought I was in pretty good shape—what was wrong with me? The answer, of course, was "thin air." Our cabin was located at an elevation of 8,000 feet and we hiked even higher than that every day.

Someone explained to me that oxygen is 45% less dense at that altitude, which explains why I was gasping! Things that were easy to do back home became a lot harder in such thin air.

AS I THOUGHT about that fact, I realized why my writing hadn't been going so well. Scripture sometimes compares the Holy Spirit to air or wind. Jesus promised His disciples that they would receive power from on high when the Spirit came, and indeed, they were transformed when the rushing wind from heaven blew on the Day of Pentecost and they were filled with the Holy Spirit.

We all need the Holy Spirit's power to accomplish the work God gives us to do. I sometimes forget that, and I try to write on "thin air," relying on my own experience and knowledge instead of on the Spirit's inspiration. No wonder I huff and puff! My prayer, as I return to my desk and my work-in-progress this week is summed up in one of my favorite choruses: "Spirit of the living God, fall afresh on me . . ."

HOW'S THE air where you're serving our Creator? Are you huffing and puffing on your own, or allowing the wind of the Holy Spirit to empower you?

Prayer

Lord Jesus, so often I try to accomplish Your work on my own abilities—and then I wonder why I run out of strength. Fill me anew with Your Holy Spirit, I pray. Help me to remember that You desire us to work with You, not for You.

NINETEEN

THANK YOU, MOM!

"Her children arise and call her blessed...Charm is deceptive, and beauty is fleeting; but a woman who fears the Lord is to be praised." Proverbs 31: 28, 30

YOU CAN DO some amazing things in your lifetime if you live to be ninety years old—and my mother, Virginia "Jinny" Davis, has. We celebrated her ninetieth birthday with a gala party with her family, friends and neighbors. I wouldn't be an author if it weren't for my mom. Nor would I likely be a Christian. She has had a powerful influence on my love of books and on my faith in Christ.

Among my first memories are of Mom reading bedtime stories to me and my two sisters, Bonnie and Peggy. Books always filled our home. Trips to the library—even if it meant walking a mile or more—were routine. Mom's love of books began when she discovered the public library as a girl during the Great Depression.

It's probably not an exaggeration to say she read every novel in her town's tiny library. The sympathetic librarian even let her borrow books from her personal collection.

Although a career as a librarian would have been her first choice, Mom never could have afforded a higher education after high school if it's weren't for WWII. She won a scholarship to become a registered nurse and became the first woman in her family to have a professional career.

HER LOVE of books never dwindled, and when the library in our small New York State town needed a librarian, she applied for the job. It's also not much of an exaggeration to say that I grew up in that library, doing everything from processing books and working at the checkout desk, to shelving books and reading to the children for story hour.

Within a few years, Mom transformed that library from a dark, dismal place that was open only a few hours a week, into the town's thriving centerpiece with activities for people of all ages. The local elementary school decided to hire her as their librarian, too. I'm so proud of all that she accomplished.

THROUGHOUT MY GROWING-UP YEARS, I also remember Mom sitting at her typewriter and writing short stories and poems and magazine articles. She wrote a regular column in a local newspaper for a time. I remember celebrating with her when one of her stories was accepted by *Highlights for Children*. She is still writing stories to this day. Mom showed me that if there's something you want to do—like write a story—then why not sit down and do it? I attribute my own love of books and my talent for writing to her.

Even more important to Mom than books, though, was her

faith in God. She experienced His presence during a church service as a teenager and her faith has continued to grow stronger and deeper ever since. She made sure that my sisters and I regularly attended Sunday school and church, and she modeled a life of prayer, regular Bible study, and loving God and our neighbor.

She has experienced hard times and losses over the years—a stillborn baby, a life-threatening illness, my dad's early death at age 62, my sister Bonnie's tragic death from cancer nine years ago. Mom's faith in a loving God has never wavered.

At age ninety she is a prayer warrior, rising early every day to pray for my sister and me and our spouses, her twelve grandchildren and their spouses, and her seventeen great-grandchildren, including three adopted ones, and those yet to be born. I feel her prayers holding me up when I travel and speak and when I sit down at my computer to write.

THANK YOU, Mom! You continue to be a role model and an inspiration to me, and to your 30 descendants, and to everyone you meet.

Prayer

Heavenly Father, we thank You for the godly people You placed in our lives at just the right time and in just the right place. As they have planted the seeds of Your Word in us, and nourished them into fruitful plants, help us in the same way to be a godly influence in someone else's life today.

TWENTY
PARADE OF LIGHTS

"Your word is a lamp to my feet and a light to my path."
Psalm 119:105

FOR OUR FIRST Christmas in our new community, my husband and I decided to get involved by volunteering to be marshals for the annual Parade of Lights. Our job, we were told during orientation, was to make sure everyone remained behind the orange safety cones that lined the street so no one would get run-over by the parade floats and fire engines or trampled by the marching bands. It was especially important to watch over the small children and keep them out of the road. Sound easy enough?

I thought so, too. What I didn't realize was that the organizations sponsoring the floats would be tossing candy into the audience. And that dozens of foolish children would risk getting run over in order to get that candy. My simple job turned out to be not so simple.

I started by smiling sweetly and asking the dear little cherubs to please step back. "We wouldn't want to get squished now, would we?" By the time the last float rolled past it took every ounce of willpower to keep from screaming, "GET OUT OF THE ROAD! Do you want to die for a lousy piece of candy?"

I CONFESS that when my kids were small I was a helicopter mom, always hovering over them, worrying about all the terrible things that might happen if I didn't remain vigilant. I realize now that it was because my writer's imagination was always working overtime. I could easily visualize a multitude of plot lines for my children's lives, and it was my job to make sure their stories ended happily-ever-after instead of in tragedy. It was exhausting.

I envy mothers who lack this kind of imagination, never picturing their daughter's prom date as a serial killer or their son's class trip to the museum ending up on the evening news. My mothering—like my imagination—never went off-duty.

SO HERE I was at the Parade of Lights, dressed in a glowing green safety vest, responsible for keeping the citizens of my town safe behind the orange cones for an entire city block. In the dark. With candy showering down from heaven on the giddy, over-excited children. I'm sure the floats were beautiful. I didn't see them. I'm sure the twinkling lights seemed magical. I was too busy trying to remember what I'd learned during orientation about emergencies. Because I could see potential emergencies everywhere!

. . .

THANKFULLY, none of the little darlings on "my" block got squished or trampled—although I may have come close to strangling one or two of them. Especially the kid who kept moving the safety cone into the street and insisting, "I am behind it!" But I was still imagining disasters as I lay in bed that night, trying to sleep, and I came to the conclusion that what I do for a living—writing novels—is a lot like being a safety marshal for the Parade of Lights. Here's why.

THERE ARE things in life that are very beautiful—like the parade floats. And things that can harm us—like the parade floats. The trick is in knowing where to stand.

As I used to tell my children, the safest place to be is in the will of God. Temptation, like candy, promises something sweet, but reaching for it may cost us our lives. It's my hope, my prayer, that the stories I write will not only entertain readers, but will help them see that the choices we make have consequences.

WHEN WE FAIL to stay behind the orange safety cones that God has given us in His Word—or when we foolishly try to move them—we are in danger. And to do so for something that won't bring long-lasting satisfaction is foolish indeed.

As I dream up characters and plot lines for my novels, what I'm really doing is showing readers where to stand, and what might happen if we yield to temptation. And also how blessed our lives can be when we choose to walk with Christ, the Light of the World.

SO, wherever life takes you, please remember to stay behind

the safety cones. "We wouldn't want to get squished now, would we?" Don't make me have to shout: "GET OUT OF THE ROAD! Do you want to die for a lousy piece of candy?" God has much better things planned for those who love Him.

ENJOY THE PARADE.

Prayer

"Heavenly Father, You are so faithful to give us boundaries for our lives to keep us from harm. Help us to remember that Your laws are given to us in love, so that we may live the good life You have planned for us. And help us to turn away from the glittering temptations that will do us harm.

Something More...

"Then, because so many people were coming and going that they did not even have a chance to eat, [Jesus] said to them, 'Come with me by yourselves to a quiet place and get some rest.'" (Mark 6:31)

Don't you hate it when the batteries go dead on devices you rely on like cell phones and laptops and tablets? But when we use them incessantly without taking time to recharge them, they eventually run down and stop working.

After a year of hard work, I just completed another novel, and I have to admit that my creative batteries are dead. Totally dry. Used up. It's time to take a break from writing and recharge my batteries. How will I do it? I think everyone has to discover the best way they personally recharge, but here's what works for me.

- Reading – Of course I'm always reading. But as I race toward the finish line on my manuscript, I put in such long days at the computer that I don't have time to read for pleasure. I feel like I'm all out of words! It's time to fill my head and heart with lots of new ones. I'm heading to the library and the bookstore for piles and piles of books so I can gorge myself.
- Beauty – God's creation is all around me if I take time to look, but when I'm under deadline, stopping to smell the roses just doesn't happen. My world shrinks to two rooms—office and bedroom. I

need to expand my world again and take time to notice the beautiful things all around me. I plan to enjoy daily walks and bike rides and let the beauty of God's creation restore me.

- Friends – Writing is a very solitary job. Sometimes it seems like the only people I talk to are my imaginary characters. To recharge, I need to spend quality time relaxing with real people—especially my friends and family. With plenty of feasting and laughter, I will soon be filled to overflowing, and ready to write about the relationships that are so important in all our lives.

- Quiet Time With God – Even though I have a regular morning devotional time, it often feels rushed when I'm under deadline. When I'm recharging, it's wonderful to be able to spend time just relaxing and reading the Bible along with devotional books from my favorite Christian authors. It's wonderful to take time to enjoy fellowship with God the way I enjoy being with my friends. And I know that the spiritual wisdom I'll receive from my fellow Christian writers will give me new thoughts and ideas to write about when I'm ready to return to the computer.

Unlike the Energizer bunny, we can't keep going, and going, and going. What recharges your batteries? Why not make a list of all the things you love to do to recharge? Then you'll be ready to schedule a break—even if it's a small one—to power-up for the work God has given you to do.

WEEK FIVE

"Why are you downcast, O my soul? Why so disturbed within me? Put your hope in God, for I will yet praise Him, my Savior and my God." Psalm 42:3

TWENTY-ONE
HELPLESS

"God is my refuge and strength, an ever-present help in trouble. Therefore we will not fear, though the earth give way and the mountains fall into the heart of the sea, though its waters roar and foam and the mountains quake with their surging." Psalm 46:1-3

OUR TWO-WEEK VACATION on Sanibel Island in Florida was wonderful—just the break I needed after finishing my latest novel and before starting the research process for the next. I sat in the departure lounge in the Fort Myers Airport with my husband on Saturday, thinking about all of the things I needed to do when I got home.

The inbound flight arrived, but we were told there would be a delay before we could board due to a mechanical issue. One hour stretched into two. I tried not to grow nervous as I watched the mechanics "tinkering" with something on the wing of our plane. And I was greatly relieved when the airline finally announced that we would be moving to a new gate to board a different aircraft.

AT LAST WE LIFTED OFF. But an hour into the flight, I happened to glance out the window in time to see our airplane make a giant U-turn in the sky. The flight attendants, who had just begun serving snacks and beverages, abruptly steered their carts back to the galley. Then the announcement came: "Ladies and gentlemen, the pilot has just informed us that we need to make an emergency landing due to a mechanical problem. We should be on the ground in Orlando, Florida in about 30 minutes."

No one wants to hear news like that when they're ten-thousand feet above the earth! As panic set in, I realized that I was utterly helpless to control any aspect of my life or my future. All I could do was pray—and of course, I did. Fervently! Everyone else must have been doing the same thing because the plane became eerily quiet. The next thirty minutes seemed like an eternity.

THE BOOK I happened to bring along to read on that flight was *Be Still My Soul* by Elisabeth Elliot. Her words took on new meaning as the stricken plane descended. "We have to come to Him in humility, acknowledging our helplessness and our utter dependence on Him. ... If we have given our lives to Him, we are able to accept everything that happens to us as from His hands."

We have a Savior we can trust, Elliot says. Whatever befalls us, however it befalls us, we must receive it as the will of our all-loving God.

. . .

MOST DAYS, I go about my life with the illusion that I'm in control. I can decide where and when I'll go on vacation, which airline I'll fly with, how my novels will end, and which book topic I'll write about next. But my helplessness on that airplane reminded me that my ability to control things goes only so far. Ultimately, my life doesn't belong to me, but to God, who has redeemed it through His Son.

If I've given my life to Him, then He is in control, not me. And I'm helpless to save myself spiritually, as well. If we crashed and my life ended, none of my good deeds would have any merit at all. "Nothing in my hands I bring; simply to the cross I cling."

OF COURSE, we landed safely or you wouldn't be reading this book. We got off the broken plane and were loaded onto a third aircraft an hour later. I confess that my knees felt very wobbly as I boarded.

The sick, churning feeling in my stomach grew worse. "The third time's the charm," our flight attendant said cheerfully as we took our seats. Once again, I would be vulnerable and help-less, thousands of feet above the earth, for another two-and-a-half hours.

And yet, in a strange way, I'm grateful for the reminder of God's power and my own helplessness. The new year is certain to bring many changes and challenges that I can do nothing about.

There will be many more times when I'll feel panicked and afraid and helpless. As Elisabeth Elliot says, we do have control over one thing: "You can choose to trust His faithfulness in every detail of your life."

"*When I am afraid,*" the Psalmist wrote, "*I will trust in You*" (Psalm 56:3).

. . .

IS THERE a situation in your life that makes you feel helpless and out of control?How will you react? How might you remind yourself that God is in control and can use our weakness for His glory?

Prayer

Heavenly Father, when I am worried and filled with fear, please help me to remember that my life is safe in Your loving hands. Help me to believe that everything that happens to me can be used for Your glory. Whenever feel helpless, help me to know that You are in control.

TWENTY-TWO

THE VOYAGE

"Fear not, for I have redeemed you; I have summoned you by name; you are mine. When you pass through the waters, I will be with you' and when you pass through the rivers they will not sweep over you." Isaiah 43:1-2

I ONCE HEARD a speaker compare life to a kayak trip down-river. Sometimes the waters are smooth and we can enjoy a leisurely journey, admiring the beauty all around us. But every now and then we hit the rapids and we're suddenly thrown into a mad scramble to stay afloat. As we navigate past rocks and other dangers, overwhelmed with fear, we wonder if life will ever be serene and peaceful again. Eventually the river smooths out and we sail back into calmer waters. And if we're wise, we will have learned some valuable lessons that can prepare us for the next patch of rough water. Here's what I learned on last year's voyage:

. . .

OUR FAMILY HIT the rapids when my husband suffered a heart attack. He has fully recovered now, and we're back to smooth sailing. But during those weeks of frantic paddling, I learned that life is fragile and precious. God can call us home to Himself at any time. More than ever, I want to hold my loved ones close in the coming year, and not squander a moment of time that I have with them. I need to remember which things in life are really important and which ones aren't worth fussing about.

IN MY FAITH WALK, I came into some challenging waters last year when our church hired a new lead pastor. He is a wonderful preacher, and our church has welcomed and embraced him. But he is challenging us to get out of our comfortable ruts so we can think more like Jesus and serve more like Him.

I much prefer to float in a lagoon with people who are just like me—but Jesus longs for me to reach out to those who are different, those who may be drowning in the rapids, and offer them a helping hand. Yes, the comfortable ministries I've been involved with in the past have been good ones. But for the sake of the kingdom, it's time for me to stop "doing church" and get involved with the world around me in the same way Jesus did.

MY WRITING LIFE has been mostly calm this past year. And yet . . . I have felt God challenging me not to settle for safe waters. As an act of trust, I need to take new risks and move out into deeper water. One way I've been doing that is by self-publishing an out-of-print novel of mine called *Fly Away*. It took a lot of work and required learning new things—and you know what they say about teaching old dogs new tricks!

A letter from a reader made it all worthwhile when she wrote to tell me how much *Fly Away* has blessed her. Why start a new venture when I've been successful with a traditional publisher? Why not stay in safe waters? Because sometimes complacency masks a lack of faith. I don't like change—does anyone? Yet I know from experience that my faith grows the most during times of change.

I WISH I could see around the bend in the river at what lies ahead for the future—but I can't. So, I'm choosing to sail forward into the unknown, comforted by one of my favorite verses from Isaiah: *"When you pass through the waters, I will be with you; and when you pass through the rivers, they will not sweep over you."*

Bon Voyage!

_____

Prayer

Heavenly Father, as we journey with You in our walk of faith, remind us that You are always near when we are afraid. Help us to keep walking and growing in spite of unwanted change. And bring us safely to the place
You desire us to be.

TWENTY-THREE

UNSEEN

"So we fix our eyes not on what is seen, but on what is unseen. For what is seen is temporary, but what is unseen is eternal." 2 Corinthians 4:18

I READ this verse in 2 Corinthians, recently, and it has challenged me to view life differently—so why not start today? In the verse, believers are advised to *"fix our eyes not on what is seen, but on what is unseen."* The irony makes me smile. How in the world can I fix my eyes on something that can't be seen? But I do understand what the verse means.

LIKE MOST OF US, the believers in Corinth are experiencing trouble. Instead of dwelling on their problems, they are told to trust that God is at work in a way that isn't visible. They are assured that *"what is seen is temporary, but what is unseen is eternal."*

Hmm. Does this principle really work? I decided to look back at some of the big and little troubles I've experienced over the years. Were the "seen" problems really only temporary, while God was accomplishing something else in the background, something that had eternal results?

YEARS AGO, I arrived as a freshman at Hope College filled with excitement about all the great courses I would take. But since freshmen were the last ones to register, I was frustrated to discover that the classes I wanted were all filled by the time I tried to sign up. This included Introduction to Art which I was eager to take to fulfill a college requirement. My advisor said to sign up for Introduction to Music instead, then wait for someone to drop out of the art class and switch. No one ever dropped out!

I remember being very angry at being forced to spend time studying music, which didn't interest me, just so I could maintain a B average and keep my scholarship. It seemed so unfair. But one day a handsome music major came up to me in the hallway and offered to tutor me. Thanks to him, I got an A in the course. We've been married for 47 years.

THAT'S one of the more light-hearted examples I've thought of, but of course there have been some serious "troubles" over the years. I thought my life couldn't get much worse after my husband won a job performing with the Winnipeg Symphony Orchestra in Manitoba, Canada. (Winnipeg is north of North Dakota, by the way). Thousands of miles from my family, I was stuck at home with three small children, buried beneath several feet of snow, and forced to endure sub-zero temperatures for months at a time.

Believe me, I couldn't imagine any eternal results. But that's when I sat down one day while my children were napping and decided to try my hand at writing a novel. By the time we moved back to the U.S. after eleven years in Canada, I had finished four novels (and made peace with the Canadian climate).

WHEN A NEW YEAR BEGINS, I'm taking time to reminisce about all my experiences, looking for the "unseen" blessing in each circumstance. In most cases, I can see that an eternal purpose was accomplished. In the cases where I can't, perhaps that particular story isn't finished yet. I'm amazed at God's faithfulness in every circumstance.

I wonder how different my life will be, how much less stressful, if I face any troubles that come my way in the new year with this verse in mind, knowing that *". . . our light and momentary troubles are achieving for us an eternal glory that far outweighs them all."*

Prayer

Lord God, it's so difficult, at times, to see our circumstances through eyes of faith—and so easy to judge merely by what our senses tell us. Help me to remember Your faithfulness in the past, and to trust that Your sight is far greater than mine.

TWENTY-FOUR
CATCHING THE WIND

"The wind blows wherever it pleases. You hear its sound, but you cannot tell where it comes from or where it is going. So it is with everyone born of the Spirit."
John 3:8

EVERY SPRING the youth group at our church holds a banquet where they auction off an assortment of great prizes to fund their summer mission trips. I bought a ticket for a chance to win a sailboat excursion on Lake Michigan. I've never sailed before, but I love to sit on our beach and watch the sailboats gliding gracefully across the lake, their white sails billowing. It looks like such a calm, peaceful way to travel. I never imagined I would win—but I did! Last weekend, my husband, our son Benjamin, and I claimed my prize.

LAKE MICHIGAN WAS WONDERFULLY CALM, perfect

for a first-timer like me. We set off in the afternoon with our host Bob Carlson on his sailboat named *Joy*. After a quick lesson, Benjamin served as his crew member as we navigated the channel at Port Sheldon, Michigan and sailed out into the big lake.

The voyage was every bit as serene and lovely as I had imagined it would be as we headed north on a gentle wind. I began to dream of buying my own boat and learning how to sail it.

EVENTUALLY, the time came to turn around and sail home. Except that the wind had died down close to shore where we were sailing, and we came to a halt. We drifted for several minutes, unable to catch a good breeze, going nowhere. In order to get home, Bob said we needed to steer the boat farther out into the lake where the wind was stronger.

I liked staying within sight of land where it seemed safe, but I also wanted to return home before nightfall. So, we fired up the motor for a minute and steered out into deeper water. Sure enough, within a few minutes, our sails filled once again and we began moving swiftly toward home.

I WAS AMAZED by how a skilled sailor like Bob could "feel the wind," as he put it, and use its power to go in whatever direction he chose. I recalled how Jesus compared the wind to the Holy Spirit, and I wondered if there were some lessons here on Lake Michigan for me.

I know from experience that when I labor on my own, without the Spirit's power, I get nowhere—just like our drifting sailboat. I also know the feeling of soaring with the Spirit's help and accomplishing so much more than I could ever do on my own. Why don't I learn to "feel the wind" of the Spirt and harness its power more often?

I suspect that sometimes it's because I want to stay safe near the shore instead of venturing out into deeper, more dangerous waters. I feel more in control that way. What might God ask me to do if I surrendered control to Him?

WITH THE WIND'S POWER, we got to our destination much faster than we ever could have by rowing. And oh, what a glorious feeling it was when the wind filled our sails and we began to move!

I imagine it was how Peter and the other disciples felt on the day of Pentecost when the Holy Spirt blew on them like a mighty, rushing wind. The same power that changed the world is available to us. All we have to do is let it fill our sails.

Prayer

Heavenly Father, it's tempting to sail through our days without a sense of Your purpose. It's also tempting to row on our own, without seeking Your help. Fill us with Your Spirit like a mighty wind so we will experience Your presence and accomplish Your purpose for our lives.

TWENTY-FIVE
WHEN PLANS CHANGE

---

*"So do not fear, for I am with you; do not be dismayed,
for I am your God. I will strengthen you and help you; I
will uphold you with My righteous right hand."*
   Isaiah 41:10

MY HUSBAND and I planned our summer vacation months
ago. All spring, we've looked forward to exploring the wilds of
Michigan's Upper Peninsula with our friends, seeing Tahqua-
menon Falls, the Pictured Rocks National Lakeshore, the
historic Grand Hotel on Mackinac Island, and taking a boat
tour through the Soo Locks.

Then a family medical emergency cancelled our plans
when my husband suffered a heart attack. We're thankful that
God answered our prayers and the emergency ended with
Ken's health being restored, but our trip will have to be postponed until next summer.

. . .

OUR CHANGE in plans has started me thinking about some of the summer vacations we took with our children when they were small. One of the most memorable was a trip from our home in Winnipeg, Canada to Colorado's Rocky Mountains, towing a borrowed pop-up trailer. We awoke after our first night of camping to find that all four of the trailer's tires had gone flat. After a trip into town to buy four new ones, we were on our way again.

Once we arrived in the Rockies, we discovered that the trailer had a broken heater, so after a few very cold nights, we changed our plans and headed south to the Grand Canyon and warmer weather.

Somewhere around Durango, Colorado, several warning lights on our car's dashboard began flashing. We made a detour to a repair shop and learned that the pop-up trailer had a faulty electrical system, which was draining our car's battery. After more repairs and a new battery, we were on our way again.

We showed up at the canyon at sunset, which is a beautiful time to arrive unless you need a campsite. All of them were full. Signs throughout the park threatened enormous fines for camping anywhere except in designated sites. And it was a long, hot drive back to the nearest town.

WEARY AND DESPERATE, we pulled into a parking lot behind a restaurant for the night. We didn't dare to "pop up" the pop-up and risk a costly fine, so we decided to sleep in our car. All five of us. In our Toyota station wagon. Our sons Joshua and Benjamin slept in the two front seats, reclining them back as far as they would go. Ken and I emptied the luggage from the back of the car, folded down the rear seat, and slept there with our daughter, Maya. I use the term "slept" very loosely.

"Dozed" is more like it as Ken and I folded ourselves around the wheel wells and tried to avoid Maya's flailing arms and legs.

ALL NIGHT LONG, I expected to hear a dreaded knock on my window, and to face an angry park ranger ticketing us for not camping in a designated area. I planned to reply, "Does this look like we're camping? If we were camping, I would be asleep in the trailer behind us, not folded like a pretzel in our Toyota!"

The long night ended without any fines. In fact, by morning, the entire parking lot was filled with cars and trailers and rumpled families just like ours. I wasn't the only one who didn't know how hard it would be to find a campsite at the Grand Canyon.

We saw a lot of beautiful sites on that trip and had a lot of fun. For Ken and me, it was memorable because of the costly tires, the new battery, the electrical work, and the sleepless night. But when we asked the kids what they enjoyed most about that trip, guess what they said: "Sleeping in the car!" One of them asked if we could do it again.

I DISLIKE CHANGE, especially when it collides with my well-laid plans. It seems as though the unplanned, unexpected changes that come our way leave a deeper imprint in our memories than when everything goes according to schedule. I will get to Michigan's Upper Peninsula another year. In the aftermath of our medical emergency, I saw how beautifully our family pulls together and shows our deep love for one another.

Our faith has been strengthened after sensing God's presence throughout the crisis and knowing that He hears and answers our prayers. In the end, that's worth much more to me than a pile of vacation photos.

. . .

WHERE HAVE you seen God at work when your plans were changed?

Prayer

Heavenly Father, we don't like change, and we sometimes fight against it. Help us to always see Your hand at work when things don't go as planned. Help us to use it as an opportunity to draw closer to You and learn to trust You in a deeper way.

Something More...

"You saw how the Lord your God carried you, as a father carries his son, all the way you went until you reached this place." (Deuteronomy 1:31)

I find that my faith is always nourished when I take time to reflect on my journey with God and think about the lessons He has taught me along the way. So, grab a pen and a piece of paper and try this exercise with me: Describe your life's journey in ten words.

Now take a few minutes to reflect on each word that you listed. Why did you choose that particular one? List some of the events or circumstances that made you choose it.

Some of those memories are probably happy ones, while others are very painful. Our lives are always a mixture of joy and sorrow. But as you reflect back, can you now see God's hand at work in the hard times? Where did you feel the Holy Spirit's power and guidance? When did you sense Christ's love?

In the midst of our struggles, we often can't see a reason for our pain. It's only when we take a longer view of our lives that we realize God was with us all along, working in all of our circumstances for our good and for His glory.

. . .

Remembering gives us hope. God was with us. He is with us now. And He will be with us in the future until the end of our days.

WEEK SIX

"Praise the Lord, O my soul; all my inmost being, praise His holy name. Praise the Lord, O my soul, and forget not all His benefits." Psalm 103: 1-2

TWENTY-SIX

REMEMBERING DR. MARTIN LUTHER KING, JR.

"Anyone who claims to be in the light but hates his brother is still in the darkness. Whoever loves his brother lives in the light, and there is nothing in him to make him stumble." 1 John 2:9-10

I WAS seven or eight years old, growing up in a village in rural New York State, when I learned my first lesson about racism. My mom, my two sisters, and I had traveled to a nearby city on a shopping trip. For a treat, we went to the lunch counter at the dime store for grilled cheese sandwiches and French fries.

That's where I saw the two signs, one labeled "Whites Only," the other "Coloreds." I asked Mom about them. Her impassioned explanation made it clear to my young heart that discrimination on the basis of race was a terrible injustice.

AS I GREW OLDER, news of the Civil Rights Movement

appeared on the front pages of the newspapers and in nightly newscasts. I knew that a great war was being fought, with soldiers and guns and the deaths of innocent civilians. The battle divided our nation.

I was a teenager when Dr. Martin Luther King, Jr. was assassinated, his death the result of hatred and racism. In spite of all the laws and amendments our government had passed, the injustice I had glimpsed as a child continued. Sadly, some fifty years later, it still continues.

I RECENTLY READ an eye-opening book entitled *I Will Not Fear* by Melba Pattillo Beals. It details her lifelong battle against racism and how it shaped her deep faith in God. In 1957, fifteen-year-old Melba was one of nine African American students chosen to integrate Central High School in Little Rock, Arkansas.

Her account of the abuse and torture she suffered at the hands of her fellow students and their parents is chilling. It required faith and enormous courage for Melba and her family to endure harassment, violence, and death threats on a daily basis, simply for the right to attend school.

MELBA MET Dr. King during that time and poured out her suffering and fear to him. He listened kindly, then told her that perhaps God had assigned this task to her. "You're not doing this for yourself," he said. "You are doing this for generations yet unborn."

His words were life-changing. Melba writes, "I had been waiting for white students to change, extend kindness, and welcome me, when maybe it was my task to change." She became a warrior for God, setting aside her own comfort to serve Him.

After one year of forced integration, the Little Rock school board decided to close Central High School and open a private, all-white school rather than educate their children alongside African Americans. But Melba and the others had made history. In 1999, she and the other eight Little Rock students were awarded the Congressional Gold Medal for their role in the integration of Central High School.

TODAY, Dr. King's words to Melba inspire me. What task requiring courage and faith might God be asking of me? Would I be willing to suffer injustice for the sake of generations yet unborn? The early Christians suffered much more than I will ever have to endure as they spread the Gospel throughout the world. Dr. King's advice to Melba reminds me of God's words of encouragement to the early Christians, and to me: "...let us run with perseverance the race marked out for us. Let us fix our eyes on Jesus...who, for the joy set before Him, endured the cross, scorning its shame..." (Hebrews 12:1-2)

Prayer

"Heavenly Father, Your Kingdom is built on love, beginning with Christ's example of sacrificial love for us. Show me, Father, all of the places where I fail to live up to His example. Teach me to love the way that You love us.

TWENTY-SEVEN
A CLEAR VIEW

"Have mercy on me, O God, according to Your unfailing love; according to Your great compassion blot out my transgressions. Wash away all my iniquity and cleanse me from all sin." Psalm 51:1-2

THE AZALEA BUSH outside my living room window puts on a glorious show every spring. I can see it from my favorite living room chair where I sit for my quiet time every morning. I can also see how dusty and rain-streaked my windows are after the long winter months.

Recently, when the temperature climbed to nearly 70 degrees, I got out the buckets and rags and window cleaner to tackle the job. The window glass is divided into dozens of tiny panes that have to be individually washed, making the task . . . well . . . a pain!

. . .

YOU KNOW that great feeling you get when you tackle a hard job and can immediately see the results? That's how I felt when I finally stood back to proudly view my finished windows. It seemed as though there was no glass in the window frames at all!

THEN I GOT up the next day.

THOSE WINDOWS FACE EAST, and as the brilliant sunlight streamed into the room it revealed every streak and smudge and swirl mark I had made. The mess hadn't been visible until the light shone directly on it. It was an appropriate lesson for me. I can delude myself into thinking I'm a pretty good Christian on the outside, all cleaned up and looking good —until Christ shines His light and reveals my spots and streaks.

THAT'S EXACTLY what happened when I spoke without thinking and my words came out in a way that hurt a dear friend. Words are my livelihood and I had used them carelessly. *"If anyone considers himself religious and yet does not keep a tight rein on his tongue, he deceives himself and his religion is worthless"* (James 1:26). Just like a dirt-streaked window.

I'M NOT AS SQUEAKY-CLEAN as I think I am. Unless I allow the Light of the World to change me, I'll remain as flawed as my windows, as filthy as my pile of cleaning rags. I've asked my friend for forgiveness. And I'm praying that from now on, the Holy Spirit will help me to *"be quick to listen, slow to speak"* (James 1:19).

Prayer

Heavenly Father, today I pray King David's prayer when he saw the ugliness of his sin: "Have mercy on me, O God, according to your unfailing love . . .wash away all my iniquity and cleanse me from my sin." Thank You for washing me clean through Christ's sacrifice.

TWENTY-EIGHT

THE ENDURING FEAST

---

*"It was just before the Passover Feast. Jesus knew that
the time had come for Him to leave this world and go to
the Father. Having loved His own who were in the
world, He now showed them the full extent of His love."*
John 13:1

WHEN THE FEAST of Passover comes in sight, my Jewish
friends, who call it Pesach, get busy cleaning their houses in
preparation, careful not to leave a single crumb of leaven. They
even vacuum their sofa cushions, something I probably should
do more often.

The table will be beautifully set with all the traditional
items in place. Family and friends will gather for this annual
dinner that typically lasts several hours. They will remember
how their ancestors, the Israelites, were once slaves in Egypt.

They'll relive the ten plagues and the nation's miraculous

deliverance from slavery. They'll sing joyful songs to celebrate God's faithfulness.

JESUS CELEBRATED the Feast of Passover with His disciples on the night He was betrayed. He broke the traditional unleavened bread and lifted the ritual cup of wine saying, *"This is my body, broken for you...This is my blood, shed for you...do this in remembrance of me."*

His closing prayer is recorded for us in John 17: *"Father, the time has come. Glorify your Son, that your Son may glorify you."* Then Jesus walked with His disciples to the Garden of Gethsemane.

I MARVEL at how the Passover Feast has endured. It began with Moses on that long-ago night in Egypt and is celebrated some 3,400 years later. God's people have also endured, just as He promised: *"Only if the (sun, moon and stars) vanish from my sight,"* declares the Lord, *"will the descendants of Israel ever cease to be a nation before me"* (Jeremiah 31:36).

Pharaoh and his pagan gods are gone, leaving only ruined temples and tombs. The Romans, who crucified Jesus and built impressive cites, are gone too. None of Israel's neighbors worship Baal or Dagon or Molech as their ancestors did.

Yet the Jewish people and their faith in the God of Abraham survive, nearly unchanged. And so does our Christian faith, some 2,000 years after Jesus died for our sins on Passover.

EACH YEAR before celebrating the feast, I love to reread the story of Christ's final Passover meal and the lessons He taught us that night (John 13-17). He began by washing His disciples' feet, saying, *"I have set you an example...no servant is greater than his master."* He commanded us to love one another saying, *"By this all men will know that you are my disciples, if you love one another."*

He told us that His Father's house had many mansions and that He was going to prepare a place for us. He promised to send the Holy Spirit to empower us. And He gave us the beautiful picture of the vine and the branches, encouraging us to bear much fruit for His Father's glory. He ended by praying for us: *"May they be brought to complete unity to let the world know that you sent me..."*

COMMUNION IS our celebration feast when we remember Christ's sacrifice. We begin by searching our souls for every speck of sin. We go to the Lord's table to partake of His body and blood in the bread and wine.

We leave the covenant meal cleansed, free from slavery to sin, empowered to bear fruit as He commanded. And we leave with a sense of peace, knowing that the Pharaohs and rulers of this world won't last, but God's kingdom will endure for all time. *"Take heart!"* Jesus told us on that long-ago Passover night. *"I have overcome the world."*

Prayer

Heavenly Father, I thank You that You are a God of miracles, a

God of resurrection power. Help us to remember and believe that You are at work in our lives every day. Help us to walk in Your strength and power today.

TWENTY-NINE
UNDERWATER EXPLORERS

"May the favor of the Lord our God rest upon us; establish the work of our hands for us—yes, establish the work of our hands." Psalm 90:17

I ATTENDED a presentation of The Michigan Shipwreck Research Association, a wonderful group of divers who search for sunken ships in the Great Lakes and it inspired me to include a shipwreck in my upcoming novel. This is exciting stuff!

These shipwreck experts start their adventures the same way I start a novel—by doing research. They comb through piles of public documents, newspaper reports and eyewitness accounts to narrow down the wreck's possible location. They search photos and drawings for the ship's distinguishing details, such as size and profile.

This research phase can be a treasure hunt in itself! But if they do their job well, the expedition has a better chance of success when the exploration phase begins.

EXPLORATION INVOLVES CREATING an imaginary grid over the suspected area of the wreck and slowly sailing back and forth, using sonar to detect a sunken ship on the bottom of the lake. Scanning for hours and hours, days on end, sounds tedious to most people, but I sensed the experts' excitement in this step of the search, too.

It requires expertise to examine the grainy sonar pictures and interpret the findings. And when a sunken ship was finally spotted, everyone celebrated.

I SUPPOSE most people would find my job tedious, sitting at a computer day after day, typing page after page, chapter after chapter until my novel is finished. While it appears to be boring, it takes expertise to create a story and get the words precisely right. And wise authors also celebrate their successes, big and small.

THE LAST PHASE of underwater discovery is obviously the most enjoyable for these veteran divers. Armed with cameras and scuba equipment, the team finally has a chance to dive on the site and explore the wreck.

I watched in fascination as ghostly images of these once-stately ships appeared on the theater screen, encrusted with shells, lying in their final resting places. I listened to the dramatic stories of their demise, usually due to violent storms. The divers became underwater detectives, solving the mystery of why and how each vessel sank, and where the ship and its crew came to their final end.

On one of the deeper dives, the team could spend only 30 minutes exploring the wreck before making the nearly two-hour journey back to the surface, pausing to adjust to the changing pressure and avoid the deadly bends.

I marveled at such disciplined devotion! Why do these divers do it? Since removing treasure from these wrecks is strictly forbidden, why make such a huge commitment of time and energy and finances to explore a sunken ship?

I SUSPECT that the thrill of diving and solving a century-old mystery are rewards in themselves. But sometimes there are other surprises, too. In the audience on Saturday night was a gentleman who had been ten years old when he lost his father in the wreck of the *William B. Davock*, sunk during a storm on Lake Michigan seventy-five years ago. His father's body was never recovered.

Thanks to the work of these divers, the now-elderly gentleman was able to see images of his father's final resting place and find closure after all these years. He sailed with the dive crew to the site on Lake Michigan and placed a memorial wreath in the water above his father's grave.

I RETURNED HOME from the program pondering why I write. There is some monetary gain, to be sure, but for me it's also about the thrill of discovery and the satisfaction of seeing the results of my hard work and discipline in book form. Most of all, it's about the joy I experience whenever I learn that one of my stories has touched someone's life.

I easily understood the joy those dedicated divers from the

Michigan Shipwreck Research Association felt when they saw the tears of an eighty-five-year-old man who had waited a lifetime to find his father.

GOD HAS GIVEN each of us a job to do, along with all of the gifts and talents we need to accomplish it. When we do His work joyfully and for His glory, serving others in His name, the rewards we will receive in return will be beyond all of our expectations.

Prayer

Heavenly Father, so much of the work we do seems tedious, and we often don't see any results from our labor. Help us to see that each task can bring You glory when done with joy and in Christ's name, even washing dishes or sweeping floors.

THIRTY
SPRING THAW

"Create in me a pure heart, O God, and renew a steadfast sprit within me. Do not cast me from Your presence or take Your Holy Spirit from me."
Psalm 51:10-11

ONE SPRING MORNING, I saw a small robin in our garden. I don't know where these red-bellied birds go for the winter, but suddenly they were back. A sure sign of spring.

So, I decided to look for other signs as I took my morning walk. Some trees now had buds. Green shoots were poking up from the cold ground along with a few brave crocuses. The ugly patches of dirty snow were nearly all melted away. And ice no longer covered the nearby lake. These early signs of renewed life meant that warmer weather and summer gardens couldn't be far away.

. . .

MY SEARCH for new life outdoors made me want to look for signs of it inside, too—not in my house but in my soul. Winter settles over the northern hemisphere each year because the earth gradually tilts away from the sun. Spring returns once the earth tilts back again.

That means spiritual winter must come when I become so busy and distracted that I subtly move away from God, the Source of life. Springtime reminds me to thaw any ice that has covered my heart and draw close to Him again.

JESUS WARNED that in the last days, *"Because of the increase of wickedness, the love of most will grow cold"* (Matthew 24:12). And He warned Christians in Revelation that *"You have forsaken your first love . . . you are neither cold nor hot."*

IT'S time to melt the snows of complacency and look for signs of spiritual life, the same way I searched for it outdoors this morning. Am I becoming more Christ-like every day? Do others see signs of change in me?

The Bible says we're supposed to continue growing throughout our spiritual journey until we *"become mature, attaining to the whole measure of the fullness of Christ"* (Ephesians 4:13).

THE BEST WAY I know to measure growth is to look for fruit in my life, using the familiar list in Galatians 5:22 as my guide: Am I becoming more loving—or becoming a permanent grouch? Am I increasingly joyful, no matter the circumstances

—or do I keep reciting the same litany of complaints and excuses?

Does the peace of God fill me—or do I continue to worry and fret? What about kindness, goodness, faithfulness, gentleness? If these still aren't part of my everyday personality, shouldn't they at least be peeking through the surface by now as signs of Christ's life in me? And how about self-control?

They say the best test for this is when someone cuts you off in traffic. Or when family members frustrate you—again.

IT WILL SOON BE time to clean out my flowerbeds, prune the dead branches, and cultivate my vegetable garden and plant new seeds. This year, it's my prayer that these springtime chores will remind me to remove the dead weeds from my heart and cultivate spiritual fruit in my soul.

Which one of these Fruits of the Spirit do you most want to cultivate this spring? How might you take the first step?

Prayer

Lord Jesus, show me all of the ways in which my love for You has grown cold. Search my heart, and show me where my life fails to produce the fruit of Your Spirit. Change me day by day until I become more like You.

Something More...

*"For God, who said 'Let light shine out of darkness,'
made His light shine in our hearts to give us the light of
the knowledge of the glory of God in the face of Christ."*
(2 Corinthians 4:6)

Once a year, I go to the doctor for my annual checkup. She
runs diagnostic tests to make sure my body is healthy and
running smoothly. It occurred to me after my last checkup, that
we also should perform spiritual checkups to make sure our
walk with Christ is strong and healthy. One way we could do
this is to test how well the Fruit of the Spirit is growing in our
lives.

Take a few minutes to read Galatians 5:16-26. It tells us
what a healthy spiritual life should look like and contrasts it
with our old, sinful nature. First, let's examine ourselves for
signs of "sickness." These include:

- *Impurity*
- *Idolatry*
- *Hatred*
- *Discord*
- *Jealousy*
- *Fits of rage*
- *Selfish ambition*
- *Envy*

Let's take time to think about each one, and silently allow the
Holy Spirit to convict us of their presence. Then ask for
forgiveness and healing.

. . .

Now, let's check for signs of spiritual health. Christ desires that we "bear much fruit," and here's what He's looking for:

- *Love*
- *Joy*
- *Peace*
- *Patience*
- *Kindness*
- *Goodness*
- *Faithfulness*
- *Gentleness*
- *Self-Control*

Meditate on each of these for a moment, and rate how you're doing on a scale of 1 to 10. Again, ask the Holy Spirit for wisdom.

My doctor always gives me suggestions for improving my health before I leave—things that usually require discipline and hard work. It also requires discipline to become more like Christ, but thankfully, we can ask the Holy Spirit to help us.

What do you need His help with today?

WEEK SEVEN

"I love you, O Lord, my strength. The Lord is my rock, my fortress and my deliverer; my God is my rock in Whom I take refuge." Psalm 18:1-2

THIRTY-ONE
MULE-HEADED STUBBORNNESS

"...how often I have longed to gather your children together, as a hen gathers her chicks under her wings, but you were not willing." Matthew 23:37

I'VE HAD my stubborn moments. Times when I've refused to do what I'm asked. When I've folded my arms and refused to budge. An incident in seventh grade art class comes to mind. The teacher assigned a short research report on any famous artist we chose.

I liked art class. I liked our teacher, an exotic woman who wore her hair in a chignon and dressed in Bohemian clothes and seemed wildly out-of-place in our boring, conventional village. Writing came easily to me. The report would have been an easy A and I was an A student. But for reasons I still don't understand, I didn't do the assignment.

. . .

WHEN MY CHILDREN used to turn stubborn, I would get angry. When my husband turns stubborn, I get frustrated. But when a character in a novel I'm writing becomes uncooperative, I'm baffled. I know, I know, I created these "people." They exist only in my mind. How can they turn rebellious? Aren't I in charge?

Well, in a word . . . no. Once I've created them along with a resume of their likes and dislikes, quirks and fears, family histories and dreams, they become "real." If I try to make them do something "out of character," it rings false. They have a right to turn stubborn.

HAVE you ever read a story where the main character does something that doesn't feel right? Something that makes you want to throw the book across the room in frustration and vow never to read a book by *that* author again?

I suspect that the character did refuse to do what the author wanted but was forced to comply against her will.

ONE CHARACTER who turned against me and my well-plotted plans was Kitty from my Civil War novel, *A Light to My Path.* She was a plantation slave who was supposed to escape. I had done tons of research about the Underground Railroad that I was eager to use.

Grady, a fellow slave who she loved, was escaping with her. Conditions were perfect for a night-time getaway. But when the "now or never" moment came, Kitty refused to go. Grady left without her. And I was left with a plotting dilemma.

. . .

I COULD HAVE FORCED Kitty to go, and maybe it would have turned out okay. Or maybe readers would have thrown my book across the room. From the moment I created Kitty, she was beaten down by her life of slavery. Her real name was Anna but her spoiled mistress renamed her and forced her to pretend she was a cat.

Kitty was too terrified of the consequences to ever disobey. Slaves were chased down and mercilessly whipped for escaping. I researched the mosquito-filled, alligator-infested swampland on her escape route, and believe me, even the bravest soul might have refused. Kitty was not brave. To run away would have been completely out-of-character for her.

MY SEVENTH-GRADE ART teacher was very surprised when I failed to turn in my paper. It was so out-of-character for me as an A student that she believed she had lost my paper. She asked if I still had the rough draft. Of course, I didn't. I would like to say that I confessed—but I didn't. She asked if she could give me a B for the assignment and I agreed. I feel the guilt and shame of my deception to this day. I hope I've developed more honesty and integrity as I've matured in my Christian life.

The Apostle Paul writes in Galatians 2:20, *"I have been crucified with Christ and I no longer live, but Christ lives in me."* I hope it would be out-of-character for me now to behave in an un-Christ-like way. I long to be true to His character in all of the decisions and choices I make. To do otherwise after the price He paid as the Author of my salvation, would be sheer, mule-headed stubbornness.

Prayer

Lord Jesus, forgive us when we foolishly continue in our stub-born, mule-headed ways. Remind us again of the price You paid on the cross so we can be forgiven. Help us to yield to Your work in our lives until we become more like You.

THIRTY-TWO

KING HEZEKIAH'S SEAL

"In everything that [Hezekiah] undertook in the service of God's temple and in obedience to the law and commands, he sought his God and worked wholeheartedly. And so he prospered."

2 *Chronicles* 31:21

IN DECEMBER 2015, Archaeologists digging near Jerusalem's Temple Mount found a stamped clay seal that once belonged to the biblical King Hezekiah. As my readers know, I "wrote the book" on King Hezekiah—three books, in fact, and two more on his son King Manasseh. I used stories from the Old Testament along with my own research to create the five-book *"Chronicles of the King"* series about King Hezekiah's life.

The clay seal that the archaeologists found was stamped with his name: Hezekiah son of Ahaz. It had once been used to seal a papyrus scroll, a document that was probably signed by

Hezekiah himself. Archaeologists discovered it in a section of ancient Jerusalem where the king's palace once stood.

I LOVE KING HEZEKIAH! This descendant of King David and ancestor of Jesus Christ ruled from about 715 to 686 BC. And what a life he lived! A contemporary of the prophets Isaiah and Micah, he lived through the exile of Israel's ten northern tribes by the brutal Assyrians.

In fact, so many refugees fled to Jerusalem that Hezekiah enlarged the city and built a new wall around it for protection. A portion can still be seen in Jerusalem's Old City.

Hezekiah also dug a tunnel beneath the city to safeguard his water supply from the Assyrians, bringing water from the Gihon Spring to the newly built Pool of Siloam. He was in such a hurry to finish that his workmen began tunneling from both ends and met in the middle, an engineering marvel. It still carries water (and tourists) beneath Jerusalem.

WHAT I LOVE MOST about King Hezekiah, and what inspired me to write all those books about him, was his faith—his imperfect, often wavering, but true-to-the-end faith. I was intrigued by the fact that his wicked father, King Ahaz, sacrificed his sons to the pagan god Moloch, yet Hezekiah launched a religious revival in the first month of his reign, purifying the temple that his father had desecrated.

He invited everyone to return to God and celebrate Passover, which hadn't been kept in decades. Hezekiah's faith grew as he faced trials.

When the Assyrians first attacked, he asked Isaiah to pray for him. When they returned a second time, he went up to the Temple and bowed before God himself, asking Him to save

Jerusalem so that all the kingdoms on earth would know that He alone is God.

HEZEKIAH'S NEWLY-DISCOVERED seal depicts a winged sun. Several news stories questioned his use of a non-Jewish symbol. But knowing what I do of his life, I think it's a perfect symbol. Hezekiah became seriously ill, and Isaiah told him to get his house in order because he was going to die.

Hezekiah prayed and God graciously granted him fifteen more years to live. As a sign that Hezekiah would indeed get well, God "gave wings" to the sun and caused it to briefly retreat backwards.

A FEW YEARS LATER, the Assyrians surrounded Jerusalem and demanded Hezekiah's surrender. Isaiah convinced him to trust God, promising that He would save the city. During the night, the Angel of Death killed 185,000 enemy troops and *"the next morning—there were all the dead bodies!"*

God's salvation from the Assyrians appeared as the sun was rising—just as, centuries later, our salvation through Hezekiah's descendant Jesus Christ would come at dawn on Easter morning.

FOR A WORLD that believes scripture is made up of fables and fairy tales, that its stories and people are fabricated and embellished, Hezekiah's newly discovered seal offers proof to those who doubt, that God's word is Truth.

Prayer

Heavenly Father, thank You for giving us the Bible—Your Holy Word—to study and learn about You. And thank You for Jesus, the Word made flesh. Send Your Holy Spirit as we read and study scripture, and bring the words to life so we can know You more and serve You better.

THIRTY-THREE
A QUIET FAITH

---

*"He has committed to us the message of reconciliation.
We are therefore Christ's ambassadors, as though God
were making His appeal through us."*
    2 Corinthians 5:19-20

WHEN I THINK of the many Christian women who've
inspired me, I always think of my paternal grandmother. I used
to spend a week or two with her during summer vacations
when I was a girl, and even though we were both eager to start
each day together, Grandma always spent time with God first,
reading her well-worn Bible and praying. Her faithfulness
made a deep impression on me.

SUNDAY WAS the Lord's Day, and I loved going to church
with her. She was a lifelong church member and a gifted
pianist, playing for worship services and singing in the choir.

My dad sang in the choir too, and thanks to Grandma, he had a perfect record of Sunday school attendance up to the day he enlisted in the U.S. Navy at age 18 to fight in World War II. He was Grandma's only child, and I believe her prayers kept him safe during those years. As scripture says, *"The prayer of a righteous man is powerful and effective"* (James 5:16).

Grandma was a teetotaler her entire life. She joined the Women's Christian Temperance Union (WCTU) when she was 16 and took the pledge to never touch a drop of liquor. Following the motto, "Lips that touch liquor shall not touch ours," young temperance women vowed never to court or marry a man who used alcohol. Grandma married my grandfather when she was 25 and I never saw him drinking alcohol, either.

WHILE RESEARCHING one of my novels, I came across some fascinating information about the WCTU and it gave me even more admiration for my grandmother. I decided to feature this women's organization in my novel, *Though Waters Roar*.

The Woman's Christian Temperance Union was started in 1874 by a group of women who had firsthand experience of the evils of alcohol, often from family members such as their husbands, fathers or sons. At that time in America there was one saloon for every 300 people. In some towns, bars outnumbered all the schools, libraries, hospitals, theaters and parks—added together.

The ladies of the WTCU vowed to do something about it. They held prayer meetings and vigils outside popular saloons in all sorts of weather, and even went inside, sometimes, to shame patrons into going home to their wives and families. When the ladies succeeded in closing one establishment, they moved on to the next, doing their work "For God, for home, and for native land."

Carrie Nation, the wife of an alcoholic, took her protests a step further. She brought an axe to local train stations and smashed shipments of whiskey before the contents could be distributed. She was arrested numerous times, yet never quit.

IF I COULD GO BACK in time and relive any memory with my grandmother, I would choose the hours we spent sitting side-by-side on her piano bench, singing our way through her well-used hymnbook. How I loved to watch her soft, graceful hands caress the piano keys and hear her rich alto voice, a little shaky with age, as she harmonized with my girlish soprano.

She taught me to love those old hymns, and I still enjoy them today, especially Grandma's favorite, "What a Friend We Have in Jesus." Thanks to her, Jesus is my friend, too.

EACH OF US has an opportunity to be a godly influence in someone's life—whether it's members of our family, or the people we encounter every day at work or school. How easy it is to become so wrapped up in ourselves that we forget that we represent Christ. How God must long for us to shine His light in a darkened world.

Prayer

Lord Jesus, You desire us to have a godly influence on the people around us, just as my Grandma had on me. Remind us today that we don't need to do great things for Your Kingdom, but to simply do the small things with Your grace and love.

THIRTY-FOUR
LIVING BOLDLY

"I tell you the truth, if you have faith as small as a mustard seed, you can say to this mountain, 'Move from here to there' and it will move. Nothing will be impossible for you." Matthew 17:20

IF YOU LIVED in the age of the explorers, would you have had the courage to sail across the ocean on a wooden sailing vessel? I toured the Maritime Museum of San Diego on our trip to California, and as I stood on the deck of the *San Salvador*, a replica of a Spanish Galleon from 1542, I asked myself that question.

The ship is less than 100 feet long and only 32 feet wide. It seemed much too small to cross the Atlantic Ocean from Spain, travel around the tip of South America to the Pacific Ocean, and then sail up the California coast. But that's exactly what the early explorers did as they sailed to the New World.

Or how about setting sail on the *Star of India*, another

small, wooden vessel on display at the museum. It carried passengers from Great Britain to New Zealand in the mid-1800s on a voyage around the southern tip of Africa that lasted five months! I tried to imagine being stuffed into the cramped space below deck with my entire family in stormy seas, and wondered what drew people to immigrate to new lands at such great risk.

We also toured the California Science Center in Los Angeles where the space shuttle *Endeavour* is on display. What amazing courage it must take to embark on such a voyage! I can say with certainty that a trip to outer space isn't for me. I had to endure an hour and a half of stomach-churning turbulence on our flight home from California and that was adventure enough!

SO WHY ARE some people willing to "boldly go where no man has gone before" as they used to say on the TV series *Star Trek*? Where does that adventurous spirit come from? I once heard a rabbi speak on the creation story in Genesis and he had an interesting interpretation of the verse where God commands Adam and Eve to fill the newly-created earth and "subdue" it.

The rabbi believed that subduing the earth means we're supposed to use our natural curiosity and sense of adventure to explore the world and learn everything we can about it. Much like my one-year-old granddaughter who toddles around the backyard wide-eyed, examining every leaf and stick and ant with a sense of wonder.

It's part of our nature to continue to learn and grow, to explore new places, and challenge ourselves to try new things. But as we get older, we become conditioned by fear and our desire for comfort, and so we set aside our natural curiosity to remain "safe."

. . .

IF I'M NOT CAREFUL, I can lose that sense of newness and awe in my spiritual life, as well, and become what Eugene Peterson calls a mere "spectator and consumer" rather than an actively growing Christian. In his wonderful book about the life of Jeremiah entitled *Run With the Horses*, Peterson says: *"The aim of the person of faith is not to be as comfortable as possible but to live as deeply and thoroughly as possible—to deal with the reality of life, discover truth, create beauty, act out love."*

That sounds very dangerous and risky, doesn't it? Like crossing the ocean in a flimsy schooner or being launched into space. But in order to truly love others as Christ does, it's going to require fearlessness and risk-taking. We may have to leave our comfort zone and reach out to people who aren't like us.

YET IF I TRUST JESUS' promise that He will never leave me or forsake me, shouldn't I be fearless? Shouldn't I be willing to risk going boldly through life, dealing with its realities, living deeply, loving others? Will I be as courageous as the early explorers or prefer to remain safe, becoming a spiritual "spectator and consumer?"

Peterson also says, *"The only opportunity you will ever have to live by faith is in the circumstances you are provided this very day."*

AS YOU AND I look around at the circumstances we find ourselves in today, are we willing to step out boldly and live by faith? Jesus said, *"I tell you the truth, if you have faith as small as a mustard seed, you can say to this mountain, 'Move from here*

to there' and it will move. Nothing will be impossible for you."
Let's move some mountains today!

———

Prayer

*Heavenly Father, sometimes we are so afraid to risk living
deeply and loving others. Help us to remember that You provide
the courage and faith to do the work You have for us to do—
today. Lord, give me the faith and courage to move mountains in
Your name.*

THIRTY-FIVE
LIVING STONES

"As you come to Him, the Living Stone—rejected by men but chosen by God and precious to Him—you also, like living stones, are being built into a spiritual house to be a holy priesthood, offering spiritual sacrifices acceptable to God through Jesus Christ." 1 Peter 2:4-5

EVERY YEAR IN JULY, my Jewish friends and family members commemorate one of the saddest days of their calendar year—*Tisha B'Av*. It's a day of fasting and mourning to remember the destruction of God's Temple in Jerusalem. On the ninth day of the month of Av in 586 BC, the Babylonian army destroyed the temple that King Solomon built, razing it to the ground. The surviving Jews were carried into captivity in Babylon. Seventy years later the Jews returned from exile and rebuilt God's temple.

.   .   .

BUT THIS SECOND TEMPLE—WHICH was extensively renovated in Christ's time by King Herod—was also destroyed. The Roman army demolished it in 70 AD, just as Jesus had foretold: *"I tell you the truth, not one stone here will be left on another; every one will be thrown down"* (Matthew 24:2). And in a tragic "coincidence," the second temple was destroyed on the same day as the first temple—the ninth day of the month of Av.

ONE OF THE most moving sites I've visited on my trips to Israel to do research is the place the Israelis call the *Kotel*—the wall. It's one of the last remnants of the temple from Jesus' day. A Muslim shrine called the Dome of the Rock now covers the site where both temples once stood. The *Kotel* is not part of the temple buildings themselves but is a section of the retaining wall that King Herod built to support his expanded temple platform. But it's the place where Jews and many Christians come today to pray and worship.

One thing that impressed me was the resilience of the Jewish people, who still come to pray and worship the God of Abraham after everything they've endured throughout the centuries. This half-broken remnant of their destroyed temple seems like such a fitting emblem of their unquenchable faith. God's temple is gone—and yet it isn't.

"Don't you know that you yourselves are God's temple and that God's Spirit lives in you?" (1 Corinthians 3:16). As Christians, we carry the Holy Spirit with us wherever we go. And 1 Peter 2:5 says that *"you also, like living stones, are being built into a spiritual house."*

A "living stone" is a one that has been quarried and chiseled and cut to fit a specific place in a building. Whenever I feel those deep cuts, I like to picture Jesus the carpenter chiseling away at all my rough edges so I will fit into the place He has for me in His new temple.

TOMORROW, when I remember *Tisha B'Av* with my Jewish friends, my prayer will be for each of us, as Christ's living stones, to take our place and do our part so that His temple will be rebuilt. A world in exile and captivity needs to see God's glory on display in us.

Prayer

Lord Jesus, please help me to remember that the trials you bring my way can be used by You to shape me into the person You desire me to be. Help me to be willing to take my place in Your temple, alongside Your other "living stones" so that we may bring glory to You.

Something More...

"If anyone serves, he should do it with the strength God provides, so that in all things God may be praised through Jesus Christ. To Him be the glory and the power for ever and ever. Amen." (1 Peter 4:11)

One of the things I love most about being a woman is the many different roles I've played throughout my life. I've been a daughter and a sister, a student and a teacher, a friend and a wife, a mother and now a grandmother. Oh, yes, and a writer.

Most of the time, I've felt I was in the place God wanted me to be, fulfilling His purpose for that time in my life. But I recall one time before my writing career took off, when I got distracted by the wrong things. I took a job for the paycheck and security it offered, hoping they would provide a sense of worth.

It was the worst job I ever had, so stressful it took a toll on my health! I was headed in the wrong direction, and God used those painful circumstances to steer me back to writing.

Take a moment to reflect on your place as a woman in this world. Maybe you can list all the different roles you currently play—wife, mother, co-worker, sister, friend (and don't forget child of God).

How have you found satisfaction in each of them? Which roles do you sense are part of God's purpose for you? Are there any roles that you've filled for the wrong reasons?

Are you happy with how things are right now? What would you like to change? Which steps can you take to make change happen and get on track with God's purposes for your life?

WEEK EIGHT

"Wait for the Lord; be strong and take heart and wait for the Lord." Psalm 27:14

WEEK EIGHT

THIRTY-SIX
ANOTHER WAY TO TELL A STORY

"Who will rise up for me against the wicked? Who will take a stand for Me against evildoers?" Psalm 94:16

MY HUSBAND and I and three family members recently went to see an original ballet entitled *"It is Well."* It was performed by the Turning Pointe School of Dance in Holland, Michigan. What impressed me even before the show started, was reading about the dance troupe itself. The goal of this ministry, founded in 1999, is to offer "Christ-centered, wholesome, artistically pleasing entertainment for the entire family." To accomplish this, the non-profit organization trains dancers— nearly 400 of them in the Western Michigan area—by following the motto, "preparing the dancer in body and spirit to glorify God through artistic excellence."

THE ORIGINAL PERFORMANCE I attended that night was

based on a book I had read several years ago entitled *Things We Couldn't Say* by Diet Eman. The Dutch author tells the true story of how she and her fiancé, Hein Sietsma, along with a group of their young friends in the Netherlands, risked their lives to save Jewish families after the Nazi invasion in 1940. Diet was only nineteen years old, but her Christian faith and the deep commitment to God that she and Hein shared made them willing to serve Him no matter the cost.

THEIR DANGEROUS WORK with the Dutch Resistance led to both of their arrests. Diet was imprisoned then sent to a concentration camp to await trial. In her book, she openly shares the spiritual struggles she experienced during that time and the anger and confusion she sometimes felt toward God. Yet her faith remained strong. Her fiancé Hein suffered imprisonment in multiple concentration camps during the course of the war, but his trust in God also endured. Diet was eventually released and continued working for the Resistance until liberation. Hein died in Dachau Concentration Camp in Germany only a few months before the war ended.

NOW IMAGINE this moving story set to music and interpreted by a team of creative, talented dancers. With only minimal narration, these artists conveyed all of the drama and emotional passion through movement and rhythm. We watched Diet and Hein meet and fall in love. We saw them working together to smuggle Jews out of danger. The darkness of the Nazi takeover was stunningly portrayed by a mass of dancers in simple black leotards who poured onto the stage and overshadowed the main characters, enveloping them in a gauzy black curtain. Another dancer beautifully symbolized the Holy

Spirit's presence in the concentration camp by lifting up Diet and her fellow inmates when they fell into despair and helping them raise their hands in prayer. As a writer, my medium of expression is words. This powerful experience of storytelling without words took my breath away.

I CAME HOME with the creative jolt I was seeking—and more. The performance was a vivid reminder of how each of us can make a difference by obeying God and using our gifts. Diet and Hein served in one of history's darkest hours by offering themselves to God—and every Jewish family they hid during the war survived. The dancers and choreographers developed and used their talents to bring Him glory, and the audience that night was deeply moved. We were reminded that we're called to serve Him every day, whether it's through writing or through dancing or by simply offering a cup of cold water in Jesus' name.

HEIN WROTE his last letter to Diet on a scavenged piece of paper and tossed it from his overcrowded railroad car on his way to Dachau. Miraculously, the letter was found and made its way to Diet after the war. Part of it reads: "...even if we won't see each other again on earth, we will never be sorry for what we did, that we took this stand." I wonder how God wants us to use our gifts today to share His great love with a hurting world?

Prayer

Lord Jesus, we see the darkness in the world around us, but sometimes we can't see how You would have us serve You in it. Please, open our eyes to see the places You would have us go, and the people You would have us rescue with Your love. Give us courage to give of ourselves for Your kingdom.

THIRTY-SEVEN
SEASONS OF CHANGE

"'For I know the plans I have for you,' declares the Lord,
'plans to prosper you and not to harm you, plans to give
you hope and a future'" Jeremiah 29:11

IT'S FALL, and change is on the way. I see signs of it all around me as I go for my morning walks with my husband. The trees show it first, of course, their green leaves morphing to flaming shades of yellow, orange, gold, and rust.

The park that overflowed with activity all summer is closed and shuttered for the season. Nearly all of the boats have been hauled inland for the winter, leaving the docks deserted. The boats look out of place standing forlornly on shore, sheathed in plastic blankets to weather the coming storms. Even the beach is braced for what's coming with snow-fences lined up against the winter snowdrifts.

. . .

AS BEAUTIFUL AS FALL IS, there's something in me that panics a little at all these signs, longing for everything to stay the same. In my book *Pilgrimage* I wrote: "Change is such a huge part of life that we should be used to it by now. Instead, we resist. We're tearful on the first day of kindergarten, fearful on the first day of high school, overwhelmed as we start college. A new job, a new spouse, a new baby—all of these changes are regular parts of a normal life, yet each of these milestones inaugurates enormous changes."

Is it part of my human nature to resist change, longing for everything to stay the same? I know it can't. *Pilgrimage* tells about a season in my life when I experienced too many upheavals. But after traveling to Israel and walking in the footsteps of the heroes of my faith—Abraham, Sarah, Moses, David, and Jesus and His disciples—I realized that change is God's template for our lives, not an anomaly. It's how we grow in our spiritual walk, and how our faith grows.

I returned home from my pilgrimage with these thoughts: "Change will be good for me, not something to fear. It will strip away my self-sufficiency and self-reliance and force me to lean on God, to pray more, to trust Him, and to walk in faith with the One who invented change."

THE WORLD around me is bracing for change, and I know that I must, too. Maybe God created the vivid changes of fall so we won't be so surprised when it comes into our own lives, but we'll embrace it with joy, knowing that we serve an unchanging God.

WHAT UNWANTED CHANGES are you facing today? Why not put your hand in God's, trusting that the plans He has for you will be even better than what you could ever ask or imagine?

———————

Prayer

Heavenly Father, help me to remember that a life without change would be a stunted life. Whenever I fear unwanted change, help me to remember Christ's promise: "surely I am with you always, to the very end of the age." Thank You for being with us in times of change.

THIRTY-EIGHT

APPLE PIE AND OTHER TREASURES

"Provide purses for yourselves that will not wear out, a treasure in heaven that will not be exhausted, where no thief comes near and no moth destroys. For where your treasure is, there your heart will be also." Luke 12:33

IT WAS SUPPOSED to be a fun excursion to do research for my next book, but icy rain poured from the wintry sky as our friends, Paul and Jacki, drove my husband and me through the Michigan countryside. Paul is a lifelong resident of Western Michigan and knows just about every back road and fun, out-of-the-way place on the map—and a few places that aren't on the map. "I want to show you something," he said, as we pulled into a little town I'd never heard of. "Do you like pies?"

Of course! Who doesn't? We drove past humble houses, down streets without traffic lights or sidewalks, and pulled into the driveway of a small, unassuming, brick home. The garage door stood open but there weren't any cars in it, only a nice-looking riding lawn mower and the usual clutter found in most garages, hanging from hooks and heaped around the perimeter. "Who lives here?" I asked.

Paul shrugged. "I don't know."

WE PILED out of the car and dashed through the rain into the open garage. I like to think of myself as adventurous but walking into a stranger's untended garage, uninvited, seemed odd. I expected the door leading into the house to open at any moment and for the owner to ask us what we were doing.

Two huge, ancient-looking chest freezers stood along the rear wall of the garage. Paul opened the lid of one and asked, "What kind of pie do you like? There's apple, cherry, blueberry, pecan . . . Ooo, and homemade apple dumplings!" A hand-lettered sign listed the prices.

A battered cardboard box collected the money on the honor system. "We've had these pies before," Paul said. "You just take them home and bake them. They're delicious."

He explained that this was a fund-raising effort on behalf of a local church. The women gathered together every so often like an old-fashioned quilting bee and spent the day baking in the church kitchen. The finished pies were sold out of this garage. I glanced around but didn't see any security cameras.

The entire endeavor operated on trust, and had become well known in the community and surrounding area. Everyone for miles around knew where the small, brick house was, and that the garage door would always be open. The freezers would always be filled with pies. The cardboard money box would be waiting.

I FELT like I'd stepped back through time into a kinder, gentler era. "I don't believe it!" I said. "Who does this kind of thing?" Until two years ago, I lived in the Chicago area along with six million other people. This pie-selling setup would never work there. No one would ever agree to leave their garage door open all day, and their lawnmower and other household goods unguarded, with only a flimsy door leading into their home— not to mention leaving several hundred dollars-worth of pies in unlocked freezers. And with soaring energy costs, no one would ever volunteer to pay the electric bill for two huge, non-energy-efficient freezers. So, what sort of people would ever be this generous, this trusting?

PEOPLE WHO HAD faith in God and wanted to support their church. People who put serving Him ahead of their material possessions. People who trusted that even if the worst happened and thieves broke into their home, God would somehow use the situation for His glory. People who believed that their "neighbors" included strangers they'd never met who might be in need of a pie.

JESUS SAID, *"Do not store up for yourselves treasures on earth, where moth and rust destroy and where thieves break in and steal. But store up for yourselves treasures in heaven . . . For where your treasure is, there your heart will be also."* I'm guessing these trusting, pie-selling homeowners will have a whole pile of treasure waiting for them in heaven.

WE CHOSE a plump apple pie and put a $10-dollar bill in the money box. It turned out that Paul was right—the pie was delicious!

Prayer

Lord Jesus, You've asked us to love and serve You with all our heart, soul, and strength. Show me, today, where my zeal for Your kingdom is lacking—where I'm storing up treasures on earth instead of in heaven. Help me to be more generous, loving, and kind.

THIRTY-NINE
FEARLESS

"Find rest, O my soul, in God alone; my hope comes from Him. He alone is my rock and salvation; He is my fortress, I will not be shaken." Psalm 62:5

THE REAL-LIFE SISTERS, Agnes and Margaret Smith, who inspired my novel, *Where We Belong*, had a favorite motto that continues to intrigue me. Whenever they were in danger or in a precarious situation they would say, "God knows when the end of our days will be. We have nothing to fear."

I borrowed their motto for my fictional sisters, Becky and Flora, to use whenever they find themselves in a sticky situation. I added a humorous twist to it in one scene when they are on board a steamship during a ferocious storm at sea:

Flora cried out as the ship suddenly leaned so far to one side she feared it would tip over. Her body was crushed against the wall as her bulky steamer trunk pinned her there. When the ship righted itself a moment later, Becky shoved the trunk away, freeing her.

"Are you all fight, Flora?"

"Yes, I think so." They both took a moment to steady their nerves and secure their luggage again.

Becky exhaled. "God knows when the hour of our end will be," she said in a shaky voice. "But I sincerely hope it isn't tonight."

IT'S one thing for me to be fearless when I'm sitting in my armchair by the fireplace, and quite another when my airplane hits turbulence midway over the Atlantic Ocean. Or when I get bad news from my doctor. I'm not afraid of dying—but I sincerely hope it doesn't happen yet!

We live in fearful times. The most frightening thing about acts of terror is that we never know when or where they may occur. We could be enjoying a concert; sitting in a restaurant; visiting a tourist attraction; attending an office Christmas party; sitting at our desk at work or at school. The suspense of continually looking over our shoulder intensifies the fear—which is the terrorists' goal.

MY NIECE FACED A DILEMMA. Her fourteen-year-old son wanted to take part in an event called the Life Chain. Participants line up shoulder to shoulder along a busy street and hold up signs to remind the people driving past that "Abortion stops a beating heart," or "It's a child, not a choice." It's a peaceful, pro-life demonstration that synced well with her son's passionate, Christian beliefs.

Understandably, my niece worried about fanatics or terrorists taking aim at her sweet son and plowing into him on the sidewalk. Should she let him take part? How would you advise her? It's one thing to be courageous when our own life is at stake and quite another to let our precious children and grand-children be at risk.

A FRIEND OF MINE, who is the director of an international prayer ministry, recently met with a group of Christian women from South Korea. She asked how they handled living with the daily threat of destruction from North Korea. The women responded that they didn't have time to live in fear. They were too busy preparing to flood across the border once the evil regime was finally destroyed to bring the hope of the gospel to their North Korean brothers and sisters.

SO, I've been thinking a lot about fear lately, and what the Bible has to say about it. Several favorite passages came to mind: *"Even though I walk through the valley of the shadow of death, I will fear no evil, for you are with me"* (Psalm 23:4).

"The Lord is my light and my salvation—whom shall I fear? The Lord is the stronghold of my life—of whom shall I be afraid?" (Psalm 27:1)

"So do not fear, for I am with you; do not be dismayed, for I am your God. I will strengthen you and help you; I will uphold you with my righteous right hand" (Isaiah 41:10).

THESE ARE great verses to know the next time I'm in danger. Even more, I need to know the Savior who makes those promises. If I'm ever asked to take a courageous stand for my faith, as persecuted Christians in other nations do every day, I want to be fearless, knowing without doubt that the God I know and love is with me. He knows when the end of my days will be. I have nothing to fear.

Prayer

Heavenly Father, there are so many things in this world that make us fearful—for our own safety and for the safety of those we love. Help me to remember Your great love for me and for my loved ones, so that I can walk with courage and faith in this dark world.

FORTY

FLIGHT OF FAITH

"Do not be anxious about anything, but in everything, by prayer and petition, with thanksgiving, present your requests to God. And the peace of God, which transcends all understanding, will guard your hearts and minds in Christ Jesus." Philippians 4:6-7

EVERY NOW AND then I have the opportunity to get away from my desk and travel somewhere to speak. For months, I had been looking forward to a Ladies' Brunch at a church in St. Louis, Missouri. Having decided to fly there the day before, I arrived at the airport in Chicago at 8:30 am and checked the board for my gate number: FLIGHT CANCELLED

What? I skimmed down the roster and saw that nearly every flight was labeled DELAYED or CANCELLED. "There was a fire this morning in our main radar facility," an airline employee explained. He pointed to a long line of passengers and said: "An agent will rebook your flight."

I joined the line then called Bonnie, my contact at the church. "We'll start praying," she promised.

THE LINE BARELY MOVED. When an hour had passed and hundreds of people were still lined up ahead of me, I called my husband in a panic. "Can you look into train schedules to St. Louis?" He called back to say that Amtrak was sold out until late tonight. I decided to wait a little longer before opting for the midnight train. I was chewing my fingernails.

It took more than three hours to finally talk to a booking agent, so I had plenty of time to worry. All around me, people were shouting at employees and yelling into cell phones, explaining why they absolutely *had* to get to their destinations. My stomach churned with worry.

Then it occurred to me that God was still in control. I know, sometimes I'm slow-witted about these things. Did I believe that God had called me to speak at this church? Yes. Then if He wanted me there, I would get there. And if He had another plan for the brunch tomorrow, then all the worrying in the world wouldn't make a bit of difference.

WHEN I FINALLY SPOKE TO an agent, I was calm as I explained my problem. "I can re-book you for 10:00 am tomorrow," she said.

"That's too late. I'm the keynote speaker at 9:00 am tomorrow."

"I'm sorry but I have no seats available today."

I didn't budge. "I have to be there," I repeated, still calm. "Can you book me on any flight out then re-route me back to St. Louis?" She explained that without radar, flights were landing and taking off one at a time. The chances of getting on any plane out of this airport today were grim. I still didn't budge.

"Let me look again," she said with a sigh. I listened as her fingers clicked across the keyboard. She looked up in surprise. "I do have a seat on a flight at 2:30 today—if the incoming plane manages to land here, that is." I told her to book it.

At 3:30, I was still waiting at the gate with the other worried passengers. One young man was supposed to be the best man at his brother's wedding tomorrow. Three sweet ladies from Ireland were trying to get to their relative's house. A young soldier on leave from Japan hadn't seen his wife and 4-year-old son in months. He stood up and announced: "I'm renting a car. If anyone wants a ride, you're welcome to come with me to St. Louis."

MAYBE THIS WAS God's plan for me. I decided to join him. So did the Irish ladies and the best man. "But let's check with the gate agent one last time before we give up," I suggested. And at that very moment she learned that our airplane had finally landed. "But will it be able to take off again?" we all asked. She was reasonably certain it would. Eventually. And later that evening, it did.

The brunch went well the next morning. I testified first-hand that God answers prayer, and told the ladies we should all stop worrying. Is there a moral to this tale? Jesus said it best: *"You of little faith, why are you so afraid? . . . Who of you by worrying can add a single hour to his life?"*

GOD IS IN CONTROL—AND I'm not Him.

Prayer

Lord, no matter how many times we learn this lesson and experience Your faithfulness, we always seem to forget—and to worry. Grant us Your peace, Lord, even in our most trying circumstances, so we can be witnesses to Your love and faithfulness.

Something More...

Why do worry and fear always go hand-in-hand? The enemy constantly uses these two temptations in my life. But I've discovered a handy weapon to use when I'm tempted. It's the same weapon Jesus used when the enemy tempted Him in the wilderness: The Word of God.

The psalmist wrote, *"I have hidden your word in my heart that I might not sin against you"* (Psalm 119:11). Now, whenever I'm tempted to worry or be fearful, I use these "hidden treasures" to remind me that God is faithful and trustworthy.

- *"Great is Your love, reaching to the heavens; Your faithfulness reaches to the skies"* (Psalm 57:10)

- *"Great is His love toward us, and the faithfulness of the Lord endures forever"* (Psalm 117:2)

- *"His compassions never fail. They are new every morning; great is Your faithfulness"* (Lamentations 3:22-23)

- *"Know therefore that the Lord your God is God; He is the faithful God, keeping His covenant of love"* (Deuteronomy 7:9)

- *"For the word of the Lord is right and true; He is faithful in all He does"* (Psalm 33:4)

- *"The Lord is faithful to all His promises and loving toward all He has made"* (Psalm 145:13)

- *"The One Who calls you is faithful"* (1 Thess. 5:24)

- *"Let us hold unswervingly to the faith we possess. For He who promised is faithful"* (Hebrews 10:23)

- *"Do not let your hearts be troubled. Trust in God; trust also in Me"* (John 14:1)

- *"The Lord's unfailing love surrounds the one who trusts in Him"* (Psalm 32:10)

What are some of your favorite verses? Why not write them down and memorize them so they will be stored in your heart the next time you need them?

WEEK NINE

"Yet I am always with you; You hold me by my right hand. You guide me with Your counsel, and afterward You will take me into glory." Psalm 73:23-24

FORTY-ONE
CHEERFUL HEARTS

"Rejoice in the Lord always. I will say it again: Rejoice!
Let your gentleness be evident to all. The Lord is near."
Philippians 4:4-5

MAYBE IT'S A SMALL-TOWN PHENOMENON. Maybe it only happens in this small town. I don't know, but my husband and I noticed the difference almost immediately after we moved here. The friendliness. The smiles. The way people take time to stop and chat to strangers like us.

It began with the morning walks we take every day. The path that goes past our house to the beach is a popular one with joggers and cyclists and people out walking their dogs. We were stunned by how everyone we met greeted us with a smile and a friendly "Good morning." If we stopped to watch the boats on the lake or a fisherman casting his line, we often found ourselves in a friendly conversation with a passerby. People wave if we're sitting on our front porch.

Then there was the day I ran into the bank on a quick errand, my mind distracted by dozens of other errands on my list. The teller said something to me as I handed her my deposit slip but I didn't catch it. "Pardon me?" I asked.

She smiled. "I asked how your day is going for you.'" I barely knew how to reply! But my errands suddenly seemed less urgent as I took time to chat with her about weekend plans.

MOVING to another state meant a trip to the Department of Motor Vehicles for new drivers' licenses and plates for our cars. I steeled myself for the ordeal. We've moved numerous times over the years and I knew what to expect at the DMV. The underpaid, overworked civil servants in these busy offices rarely have much to smile about. But the people in our new hometown office were some of the friendliest I've ever met.

The gentleman who gave me my vision test joked about the elderly woman who kept asking him where the focus knob was. The woman who took my driver's license photo asked if I liked it or should she take it again. And when we were all finished, the man who had spent so much time doing our paperwork smiled and said, "Welcome to our community. I hope you enjoy it here."

One of our neighbors delivered freshly-baked cookies to our door when she came to introduce herself. I didn't think people did that anymore. The clerks who ring up our order in the supermarket chat with us as if we've known each other all our lives. Other bikers stop to tell us which new trails we should try.

Strangers in the downtown farmer's market offer advice about where to buy the sweetest corn, the juiciest watermelon. A woman from one of the churches we visited came by with a loaf of fresh bread and other goodies from the town's favorite bakery. My young neighbor across the street offered to water my plants when we went away for a weekend—and I'd only met her five minutes earlier!

I CONFESS that I was very suspicious, at first. Why were people being so nice? Was it a trick? A scam? Did they want something from me? Sadly, I've built a huge wall of skepticism after living in an unfriendly metropolitan area for the past twenty-two years. But those walls are quickly toppling—and here's the latest reason why. As I was writing this morning, one of our neighbors came to the door with a beautiful bouquet of flowers. He'd just picked them from his garden. For us!

THE BIBLE SAYS, *"A cheerful heart is good medicine"* (Proverbs 17:22), which means that the people in this town are going to live long, healthy lives. In his book, *Run With the Horses*, Eugene Peterson says, "You cannot be the person God wants you to be if you keep yourself aloof from others." So I've been practicing my smile. I've decided I want a dose of God's medicine.

Prayer

Heavenly Father, I pray that the love and joy and peace that I've found in Christ will radiate from my soul for everyone to see. Help me to really notice the people I meet, and to see Your image in each one.

FORTY-TWO

THE YEAR IN REVIEW

"For the Lord God is a sun and shield; the Lord bestows favor and honor; no good thing does He withhold from those whose walk is blameless." Psalm 84:11

IT'S popular at the start of a new year for TV specials to review the past 12 months and remind us of all the events that occurred. I did something similar one January 1st and looked at my own year in review. Every morning during my quiet time I keep a journal, jotting down what I've been doing, what I'm praying for, and any insights that God shows me as I read my Bible. Sometimes it's easy to miss the miraculous in the details of daily living, but as I re-read my journal for the year, God's hand became amazingly clear.

HIS ANSWERS TO PRAYER, for instance. I began that year with many pleas for guidance as my husband prepared to retire from his job after 22 years. All the details of his retirement seemed overwhelming to me at the time, and occupied my prayers: selling our home, packing and purging and cleaning, moving to a new home in a new state, enduring financial changes, leaving friends and family behind. But here we are, settled-in and thriving in our new home, enjoying the changes, and thanking God for bringing us here. All that worry—for nothing!

There were prayers for family members too, chief among them for our son to find a job after earning his PhD that May. It was a nail-biter and the waiting seemed endless, but in God's perfect timing, a job opened up for him at the beginning of the college year, one he is now enjoying immensely. Looking back at answered prayers in the past gives me faith to believe that God will answer my future prayers too.

ON THAT JANUARY 1ST, I wrote: "A brand new year. I can't imagine what it will bring, but I'll trust in God. I long to live intentionally, to enjoy life every day, and not simply mark time on a calendar or check off a to-do list." Little did I know all the places I would go or how much I would need to trust Him!

In March I traveled on a speaking tour to the Netherlands. When I returned, I wrote: "God gave me strength and His words to speak. He is able to do more than we can ever ask or imagine." In June, I went on another speaking tour in Germany.

In my journal I recalled how terrified I used to be of public speaking and of flying. "I wonder how often my fear and doubt have caused me to miss the good things God planned for me," I wrote. "If I had remained fearful of speaking and flying, I would have missed the blessings of serving Him in these amazing places." I used to have so much fear—when all along, God held my life in His faithful hand.

AS THE YEAR drew to a close, I wrote on December 31st: "This has been a year of so many changes and new beginnings! Lord, help me to change in the days ahead and become more and more like Jesus."

When I think about it, maybe that's what the trials and challenges we face are really all about—teaching us to trust our Savior and to become more and more like Him. As a New Year begins, I pray that God will help me replace worry and fear with faith and trust in Him.

Prayer

Lord Jesus, thank You for always answering my prayers, even when it isn't the answer I expected. Help me to remember that You can see the future—and I can't. Help me to trust that You know what's best for me in every circumstance.

FORTY-THREE
LIFE LESSONS

"Jesus replied: 'Love the Lord your God with all your heart and with all your soul and with all your mind. This is the first and greatest commandment. And the second is like it: Love your neighbor as yourself.'"
Matthew 22:37-39

I ATTENDED a funeral recently for a man I didn't know well. His daughter is a friend from church, his wife a friend from book club. *"It is better to go to a house of mourning,"* scripture says, *"than to go to a house of feasting, for death is the destiny of every man; the living should take this to heart"* (Ecclesiastes 7:2). I need a reminder, every now and then, of how short my time on earth is, so I'll make every day count. Ron's funeral reminded me of some important life lessons.

1) **LIFE IS HARD—DON'T whine about it**. Ron grew

up with seven siblings and little money. To help out, he assisted his brother with his paper route so he could buy a bicycle and start his own route. Ron worked hard and finally bought a bike —and that very day a car backed over it and destroyed it.

What did Ron do? He started all over again, working to save for another bike. As an adult, he applied the same work ethic and perseverance to start his own business, slowly growing it over the years.

I admit I'm a whiner. I love telling sob stories so everyone will feel sorry for me. But the trials we face build character— and often reveal our character. Yes, life is hard...but God is good.

2) **PEOPLE MATTER.** Ron's office manager gave one of the most touching eulogies. "He was more than my boss," she said. "He was a father to me, and a friend." People were very important to Ron. Even the doorman from his condominium attended his funeral, weeping throughout the service.

Ron knew when to leave work behind and spend time with family, attending their sporting events and programs, taking vacations together. His "family" grew into a huge extended one with plenty of love to go around.

People matter to God, and therefore they should matter to me. Is my heart large enough to encompass all the people God sends my way—including the doorman?

3) **WHAT WILL Our Legacy Be?** Ron was generous with his time, his money and his possessions. He and his family chose "birthday verses," using the month and day of their birth to select a Bible passage that spoke to their heart. Ron chose 2 Corinthians 9:6-7: "*Whoever sows sparingly will reap sparingly,*

and whoever sows generously will reap generously...for God loves a cheerful giver." Ron loved buying gifts for his family and was generous to strangers, as well. His wife said she had to restrain him from over-tipping in restaurants.

Am I living a life of generosity or sowing sparingly? As I sifted through my closets and storage rooms in preparation for our move, I was struck by the sheer amount of stuff I had stashed away. Why didn't I donate it years ago?

We've heard these truths before, in many forms: Jesus' parable of the Rich Fool who needed to build larger barns for all his stuff; Lazarus and the rich man whose concern for his family's spiritual life came much too late. And remember Jesus' words about not storing up treasures on earth? There are no U-Haul trailers behind hearses.

THE LEGACY I leave behind doesn't consist of my possessions or the money left over in my retirement account after I'm gone. I'm building a legacy every day with all the seemingly minor choices I make, the priorities I choose, and the way I treat people. And when I graduate to heaven, I hope I'm remembered for showing the love of Christ to others.

Prayer

Lord Jesus, You taught us not to store up treasures on earth where they'll rust and corrode, but to store up treasure in heaven. Help me to examine my life in light of Your word. And remind me each day to love my neighbor as I love myself.

FORTY-FOUR
JUST DO IT

"Therefore, since we are surrounded by such a great cloud of witnesses, let us throw off everything that hinders and the sin that so easily entangles, and let us run with perseverance the race marked out for us."
Hebrews 12:1

A FRIEND recently told me he had an idea for a book and planned to write it after he retires in ten years. I frequently hear comments like that, often about writing or some other dream people have for the future. "Someday, I would love to..." Followed by the excuses: "My kids are involved in too many activities right now; things are really crazy at work; I don't have a calm, quiet place to write; I don't have time . . ." My advice is always the same: don't wait!

Your life will always be too busy with too many things to do. You'll never have time unless you carve out time. And the quietest, calmest place you'll ever live is in the cemetery. Harsh advice, maybe? But I learned it through experience.

WHEN I FIRST DREAMED OF writing I had a nine-year-old, a two-year-old, a newborn, and a husband who worked two jobs. I had no idea if I had any talent, and not a clue about how to get published. I simply sat down one day when my oldest child was in school and my two younger ones napped, and began to write. It didn't take long to figure out that I loved it.

The short story I thought I was writing eventually grew into a 5-book series entitled "The Chronicles of the Kings." I was hooked. And then my kids outgrew naps and life turned crazy.

I ATTENDED A CHRISTIAN WRITERS' Conference two or three years later and author Jerry Jenkins offered some wonderful advice. His sons were young at the time, and he still had a full-time job, but he said he'd promised God he wouldn't write until his children were in bed. "Of course," he added, "I sometimes have to put them to bed at 4:00 in the afternoon..." He was joking, but his point about setting priorities was exactly what I needed to hear.

My spiritual life and my family were my top priorities. But if my dream to write truly had come from God, then it needed to be near the top of my list, too.

I SET up my computer in our family room, in the middle of *Lego* creations and dollhouses and art projects, and learned to write in spite of the chaos and constant interruptions. I carried notebooks and research books to hockey practices and swimming lessons, and planned my next chapter while pushing kids on swings. I didn't know the meaning of "peace and quiet."

MY POINT IS, don't wait! Just do it! Whatever your God-given dream is, do it now while the dream is vivid and your passion burns. Chances are the urge that won't go away, the dream that won't die, is exactly the dream God has for you. It's never too soon or too late to start. Rearrange your busy life. Adjust your priorities to make room. Then—just do it! Let your only regret be that you didn't start sooner.

Prayer

Heavenly Father, one of the reasons we so often make excuses is because we're afraid. Please, show us that we don't need to fear if we put our trust in You and in the calling You've given us. Let our motivation be Your love, and Christ's sacrificial gift to us.

FORTY-FIVE
LOVE'S MAGIC TOUCH

"A new command I give you: Love one another. As I have loved you, so you must love one another. By this all men will know that you are my disciples, if you love one another." John 13:34-35

I KNEW the visit to the nursing home would be difficult. I wasn't prepared for a miracle. I went there with my friend Cathy, whose older sister suffers from Alzheimer's disease. I knew Muriel in years past as a vibrant, happy woman who enjoyed life and dearly loved her family and her Lord. It was painful to see the empty shell she has become.

She sat slumped in a wheelchair with a blank expression on her face, her eyes dead and lifeless. The other patients in the lounge looked much the same—without life, without hope. I battled tears, my heart aching for Muriel and for Cathy. I lost my older sister, Bonnie, to cancer a few years ago, and I miss her terribly. But this "living death" seemed much more tragic.

. . .

CATHY SAT down beside Muriel and gathered her into her arms for a long, sweet hug. She kissed her, and smoothed back her hair, and told Muriel her name, and how much she loved her. And even though there was no response or any sign of recognition, Cathy took Muriel's hands, and looked deeply into her eyes, and continued talking, pouring out her love.

SLOWLY, almost imperceptibly, a light came into Muriel's eyes as she began to respond to Cathy's love. She sat up a little straighter. A gentle smile lit her face. And the love I'd seen in Cathy's eyes soon filled Muriel's eyes, too.

She may not have known Cathy's name or who she was, but Muriel knew that Cathy was someone who loved her, someone she had once loved in return.

IT WAS A HOLY MOMENT. Like watching the sunrise after a long, dark night. Or watching a winter-dead tree slowly bud and blossom. Even though Muriel's mind had lost its ability to think or remember, her eternal soul knew and understood love. And for a few, precious moments, Muriel was filled with life once again.

I wanted to go around the room to all of the other patients and hug them, and show them love so they could come alive, too! But, of course, I couldn't. I had no right.

YET, isn't that what we're supposed to do? Those of us who know the beauty and joy of God's unfailing love—aren't we supposed to generously give it away to everyone around us?

Whether they respond or not? Whether they return it or not? I think of all the "living dead" people I see every day, going through life with blank eyes and hopeless expressions.

What might happen if I found a way to draw them close to me and look into their eyes and tell them how much God loves them? Could I earn the right to do that through acts of unde-served grace, and kindness, and selfless sacrifice? Might their eternal souls respond to love?

THAT'S how Jesus demonstrated His love to me when I was "dead." And because of His love, I am now alive with eternal, everlasting life. How He must long for me to freely give His love away to others.

Prayer

Lord, open my eyes, today, to see who needs to be touched by Your love. Then give me the courage and grace to love as You do.

Something More...

"The Lord appeared to us in the past, saying: I have loved you with an everlasting love; I have drawn you with loving-kindness." (Jeremiah 31:3)

I can still remember the way my grandmother looked at me when I was a child. It didn't matter what I was doing or if my clothes were dirty, or my hair messy. Whenever she looked at me, I saw love in her eyes.

Now that I'm a grandmother, I understand her unconditional love even better. My granddaughter might be saying adorable things or having a temper tantrum; she can be dressed in frills or in a stained T-shirt. It doesn't matter. My love doesn't change.

I'm convinced this is the way God sees us—with eyes of love, like my grandmother. He may not always like what we do—and He may discipline us when we need it—but our behavior doesn't alter His love for us. We have value and worth because we are His children.

So, how do you see yourself? Do you look through the eyes of our culture, letting others decide your value based on your income, or your work, or your clothes and possessions? If so, you're using the wrong measure.

. . .

Our true value and worth come from God. He showed you how valuable you are to Him when He gave His Son Jesus so you could be His child. He will never stop loving you no matter what. Do you believe that?

Stop and make a list of all the ways God has shown His love to you.

Imagine Him gazing at you with eyes of love.

Now look at yourself in the mirror and say, "I am a beautiful woman, beloved by God."

WEEK TEN

"Surely goodness and love will follow me all the days of my life, and I will dwell in the house of the Lord forever." Psalm 23:6

FORTY-SIX

CLEANING HOUSE

"Search me, O God, and know my heart; test me and know my anxious thoughts. See if there is any offensive way in me, and lead me in the way everlasting."

Psalm 139:23-24

ON THE SURFACE, my home looks neat and tidy—most of the time. But I have a few favorite closets and cupboards and crannies where I like to stuff things. You know, all those things you aren't using but don't want to get rid of, things you conveniently shove out of sight and promptly forget. Curious and unwary visitors open the doors to these hidden places at their own risk.

Unwilling to risk an avalanche or a bodily-injury lawsuit, I've been cleaning out these catch-all places. For inspiration, I watched an episode of the reality TV show about clutter. It did the trick! I'm now motivated to clean house.

The TV show taught me to divide everything into three piles: the stuff I want to keep, the stuff I can give away, and the stuff that can be thrown away. This might seem obvious but it's harder than you think.

What may appear to be junk to an observer often has great sentimental value to me—like the crafty things my kids made for Mother's Day. Or cards and keepsakes from loved ones. Or household items that I've had ever since I married, 43 years ago. (These last items come in lovely shades of avocado green and harvest gold and are probably antiques by now.)

I HAVE bravely set to work making slow but steady progress. The local landfill will be a little fuller this week. The nearby Bibles for Missions Thrift Store may earn a dollar or two from all my junk. And the trip I took down memory lane as I sifted through my possessions was sometimes hilarious, sometimes heartbreaking.

I feel lighter now, and freer. And that was the point. So, while I'm at it, maybe it's time for me to do some soul house-cleaning, too. I need to *"throw off everything that hinders and the sin that so easily entangles"* so I can *"run with perseverance the race marked out"* for me in the years ahead (Hebrews 12:1).

I HAVE a page full of New Year's resolutions I hope to accomplish in those years, copied from the January 2014 issue of *Indeed* magazine. Among them are:

- Have enormous dreams, visions, and goals.
- Give yourself to repairing and restoring His world.
- Be relentlessly merciful.

- Seek and expect miracles.
- Speak life-giving words.
- Don't wait to enter His kingdom someday; bring His kingdom to earth now.
- Heal and comfort the brokenhearted.
- Be wildly creative.
- Never, ever give up.
- Dance, laugh, rejoice, live, love.

I CAN'T KEEP EVEN one of these resolutions without God's help. And that's where my own, personal "house cleaning" comes in. I have crannies and cubby holes in my soul that are filled with junk. Things I have stuffed out of sight so I can look good on the outside. Attitudes and habits that I know God wants me to get rid of but that I haven't been willing to relinquish. Worries and fears that I've toted around for years instead of giving them to Him.

SORTING through these hidden places requires hard work and a lot of prayer. I've found that a good place to start is David's prayer in Psalm 139: *"Search me, O God, and know my heart; test me and know my anxious thoughts. See if there is any offensive way in me, and lead me in the way everlasting."* Step by step, one item at a time, my soul-closet can be emptied and cleaned and filled with good things that can be used for His glory.

Now, back to work. I have some hidden faults that need to go to the dump. And does anyone out there need a lovely, harvest-gold fondue pot?

Prayer

Heavenly Father, search me and show me the things I've been harboring in my heart—things like bitterness, unforgiveness, selfishness, and self-pity. Set me free from them and create in me a clean heart so that I can better serve you.

FORTY-SEVEN

WHICH WAY?

He led you through the vast and dreadful desert, that thirsty and waterless land...He brought you water out of hard rock. He gave you manna to eat in the desert."
Deuteronomy 8: 15-16

WOULDN'T it be wonderful if our lives had warning signs letting us know when we're heading toward danger? I spotted a sign that read "Dangerous Abyss!" while hiking in Israel, and believe me, the abyss was enormous and without guardrails to keep unwary hikers from falling over the edge.

I've been thinking about that hike a lot as I stand at an important crossroads in my life. I wish I knew which path was the right one, what dangers and challenges lay along each trail, so I could make the best choice. What if one path takes me in the wrong direction or comes to a dead end? Or an abyss?

. . .

IN SEEKING GUIDANCE, I recall my hike in Israel, where we hiked through in the Wilderness of Zin. The Israelites traveled through this same wilderness on their way to the Promised Land—and don't we all want to end up, in the place where God wants us to be? But first we sometimes have to trek through dry, difficult places.

Only a fool would head out into the trackless wilderness without a guide. And without water! The path was barely distinguishable from the surrounding landscape, at times, and it would have been very easy to wander off and become lost. The hike was challenging, the sun merciless overhead, but our guide promised us beauty—and some lessons along the way. And our first surprise was an oasis where we least expected it.

I noticed as we followed our guide that everyone stayed within sight of him. No one lagged behind or wandered away. He had our complete trust. And eventually we reached a beautiful valley, hidden in the middle of the vast wilderness. We also reached a dead end. The narrow path we had been following suddenly ended at a high, rocky cliff.

By now, we had been hiking for several hours and the prospect of retracing our steps beneath the blazing, afternoon sun had us pretty discouraged. Maybe we had gone the wrong way and our guide didn't want to tell us.

He let us rest and quench our thirst. And while we did, he talked about trusting God to lead us through our wilderness times the way we had been trusting him in this wilderness. He explained how we need a full supply of water—God's Word—stored up in our hearts during the good times so it can carry us through the bad ones.

YES, we had reached a dead end, he said. And so often when

we reach dead ends in life we panic and scramble to save ourselves, looking for a way out instead of quietly waiting and trusting God. These were good lessons to remember. But what were we going to do now at this dead end in the wilderness?

WHEN WE WERE RESTED, our guide led us closer to the face of the cliff. And guess what—he knew the way out all along. Winding up the side of the cliff were a set of stone stairs! It wasn't an easy path by any means. In fact, it was terrifying in places. I was shaking in my shoes! But after an invigorating climb, we all arrived safely on top—and there was our air-conditioned tour bus, waiting to take us back to our hotel.

Today as I stand at my crossroads, I'm trusting God to help me choose the right path. If I let Him be my guide, if I follow where He leads and stay close to His side, even when the terrain is difficult, I might find an oasis or two to refresh me along the way.

I've been delving into His Word as I prepare for my journey, making sure I won't run dry. And while I can expect His path to be challenging, I know there will be no dead ends. I will arrive safely at last—exactly where God wants me to be.

"He set my feet on a rock and gave me a firm place to stand." (Psalm 40:2)

Is God leading you through any dry, barren places? What might you learn about trusting Him in this wilderness? If you reach a "dead end," will you quietly wait and trust Him to show you the way out?

Prayer

Heavenly Father, thank You for providing for us, even when we find ourselves in desert places. Help us to see Your hand, pointing the way for us to go. Help us to trust You to lead us to green pastures for Your name's sake.

FORTY-EIGHT
EDITING—AND LIFE!

"Send forth Your light and Your truth, let them guide me; let them bring me to Your holy mountain, the place where You dwell." Psalm 43: 3

HOW LONG DOES it take to write a book? The answer is different for every author, but for me the process takes one year. Since I write historical fiction, I begin by doing research, a step that is truly fun for me. I love reading and digesting hundreds of facts and images and ideas about different time periods and pouring that information into what I call "story soup." But my favorite part of doing research is traveling to the places I'm going to write about.

DOING RESEARCH GENERATES STORY IDEAS, and the next step in the process is creation—taking all of the raw materials and crafting them into a story. I begin by creating my characters, and I even pin pictures of how I imagine them to look on a bulletin board near my desk.

This is the fun part of writing. I can let my imagination soar, using my creativity to transform historical facts and images into a story that will bring the time period to life for my readers.

I try to let the story flow freely, and I since I don't outline the novel ahead of time, I make up the plot as I go along. But I'm somewhat of a perfectionist and usually can't resist the urge to edit what I've written as fast as I write it. I often begin each writing day by re-reading yesterday's pages (which seemed so brilliant as I was writing them!) and re-working them before launching into the new writing for that day. By the time the book is finished, I've re-written and edited the story dozens of times.

I'M BLESSED to be part of a writers' critique group, sharing my writing life with two very special women—multi-published authors Jane Rubietta and Cleo Lampos. We've been meeting together for more than 21 years now, and as they critique my work-in-progress, our collaboration always makes my novels even better. As scripture says, *"You use steel to sharpen steel, and one friend sharpens another"* (Proverbs 27:17, The Message).

When my final draft is complete, the novel still isn't finished. I always print out the manuscript so I can read and edit the printed pages. Then I type those edits back into the computer for one final rewrite. By now, my deadline usually has arrived so it's time to send the manuscript to my publishing company. I always wish that this was the final step, and that I could be finished with the project and move on to writing the next novel. It isn't.

My editor gives the manuscript to several in-house readers and compiles their comments and observations, along with her own, into a long letter of things for me to consider as I re-write it one more time. I confess, I dislike this step most of all, and would skip it entirely if I could. It makes me feel the way I did in school when a project I've worked on for a long time comes back with a grade of B instead of the A+ I was hoping for.

THE TRUTH IS, we are often blind to our own faults. The characters and story are clear in my own mind because I've lived with them for nearly a year, but to an outside reader, there may be thoughts I failed to convey, or holes in the plot that need to be filled, or maybe a loose thread left dangling. Fresh eyes can see these flaws much more clearly that I can. So, in the interest of publishing the best possible book, I've learned to value these comments, even when they prick my pride and feel like unwelcome criticism.

I'VE DISCOVERED that I need other people in my Christian walk of faith, too. We Americans are proud of our rugged individualism, and that attitude can carry over into our spiritual lives if we're not careful. "Me and Jesus—that's all I need." But it isn't true.

I know how much my writing improves as I share it with trusted friends in my critique group and with my editor. And the same honest sharing of my spiritual struggles can benefit me as well.

IT'S difficult for me to let someone "wash my feet," and even more difficult to be the one to point out the need for washing to someone else, especially someone I look up to. I admire the courage it took for Nathan the prophet to confront King David after he sinned with Bathsheba. And I admire the humility and courage it took for David to accept Nathan's rebuke, knowing that it had really come from God (see 2Samuel 12).

Whether it's my manuscript or my life, I need other people to be my outside eyes, helping me stay on the right path. When I'm brave enough to pray, *"Search me, O God, and know my heart..."* (Psalm 139:23), I shouldn't be surprised when He sends a friend into my life to gently point the way back to the right path.

Prayer

Lord Jesus, we need You and we need each other. Thank You for sending people into my life to keep me accountable before You. Forgive my pride when I'm afraid to ask for help, or when I'm slow to accept their advice. Keep my feet on the right path for Your name's sake.

FORTY-NINE
DEXTER'S LOVE STORY

"This is the message you heard from the beginning: We should love one another...This is how we know what love is: Jesus Christ laid down His life for us. And we ought to lay down our lives for our brothers."
  1 John 3: 11, 16

I'VE WRITTEN about Dexter my "grand-cat" before. How he was rescued from the streets of Chicago and adopted by my daughter and her husband. How their patience and love transformed him from an aggressive, nearly-wild cat that couldn't get along with any of the other cats in the Red Door Animal Shelter, into a much-loved family member.

I've written about some of his quirks—how he likes to play kitty video games, and how he turned a worn-out, discarded shoelace into his favorite toy. Dexter has taught me some very important life-lessons.

. . .

NOW A NEW CHAPTER is being written in Dexter's life—
and in mine—as we've welcomed a new baby into our family. I
think we all wondered how this rambunctious cat would adapt
to a newborn in "his" territory, vying for his owners' attention.

We needn't have worried. Even before the baby was born,
Dexter seemed curious about the changes taking place. As each
new baby item arrived, Dexter was the first to try it out. He
carefully inspected each box and bag that was delivered. He
road-tested the stroller for safety.

AND NOW THE baby herself is here, and Dexter is her
staunchest guardian. He's careful to stay an appropriate
distance away from her, yet he sits close enough to stand watch
over her.

He sleeps on the shelf beneath her bassinet while she
sleeps, and lays beneath her swing when she's in it. He stands
near the door to safeguard her when she's in her car seat. It's
clear that he is ready to protect her from harm.

I bought my new granddaughter a stuffed toy that resem-
bles a little tree trunk with burrow-holes all around it and
stuffed animals inside—a raccoon, a bear, a squirrel, a fox, a
yellow bird. She's too young to play with it, but Dexter isn't.

He has figured out how to pull out all the animals, and he
brings them to her, piling them beneath her bassinet or carrying
them into the room where she is. Sometimes he drags the entire
toy to her side, especially if she's crying.

THIS TENDER, protective side of Dexter has shown me, once
again, the power of redeeming love. This once-unlovable cat
has not only been transformed into a wonderful pet, but now

he returns that love, showing affection to this newest family member who isn't able to show it in return.

WHAT WOULD HAPPEN, I wonder, if I demonstrated redemptive love to all the seemingly unlovable people I know? Might they be transformed as Dexter has been? Would they also learn to love others in return?

JESUS SEEMS to think it's a risk I should be taking: *"But I tell you: Love your enemies and pray for those who persecute you, that you may be sons of your Father in heaven...If you love those who love you, what reward will you get? Are not even the tax collectors doing that? And if you greet only your brothers, what are you doing more than others? Do not even pagans do that? Be perfect, therefore, as your heavenly Father is perfect"* (Matthew 5:44-48).

THANK YOU, Dexter, for showing me how love multiples once it is shared.

———————————

Prayer

Lord Jesus, You taught us so many lessons about loving others well, and yet we fail to obey You, especially when those "others" don't seem lovable. Help us to see the people around us as You see them. Help us to love them the way that You do.

FIFTY

SMALL MIRACLES

"For nothing is impossible with God." Luke 1:37

I HAVE a story to tell about one of God's small miracles. A true story. If I made it part of the plot of a novel, the "coincidence" would be unbelievable.

LAST CHRISTMAS, I attended a concert at Moody Church in downtown Chicago with two couples from our Bible study group. My husband Ken performed in the concert. Before the music started, I was talking with my friend Peggy about the pain she still experienced from a car accident a few years ago. I mentioned that my 85-year-old mother, who has a quiet, one-woman prayer ministry, had been praying for her.

A stranger seated in front of me suddenly turned around and said, "Would your mother please pray for me, too?" He told me his name was Shad—short for Shadrach—and he explained how he was also in great pain and had trouble sleeping at night. "What's your mother's name?" he asked. "If she'll pray for me, I'll pray for her." We exchanged information, the concert began, and Shad and I didn't talk again.

Every morning, my mother (who lives 800 miles away from me) faithfully prays for her daughters, sons-in-law, twelve grandchildren and their spouses, and her eleven great-grand-children—along with countless other people she hears about, like my friend Peggy. She added Shad to her list. In fact, she told me that he often came to her mind—sometimes in the night —and she prayed for him then.

Most of Mom's prayers are answered in amazing ways, but there have been some prayers that have gone unanswered for a long, long time. She rarely asks for prayer for herself, but I knew of one particular need in her life that she was trusting God to answer—and He just didn't seem to be listening.

FOUR MONTHS after the Christmas concert, I returned to Moody Church with two friends on Easter Sunday to hear my husband play for their morning service—a glorious musical experience that always makes me feel like I'm in heaven, listening to the angels sing. When Mom heard that I would be returning to Moody Church she said, "Oh, maybe you'll see Shad again. Find out how he's doing. I think of him so often when I pray."

"Impossible," I told her. "Finding him would be like finding a needle in a haystack!"

For one thing, I couldn't even remember what he looked like, since he sat in front of me the last time. And for another, the auditorium at Moody holds close to 4,000 people and every seat is filled on Easter. I found it impossible to imagine that I would cross paths with Shad again, especially since I would be sitting in a completely different part of the auditorium this time. But for Mom's sake, I did look around half-heartedly that morning, eyeing the name tags that ushers and some church members wore, looking for one that said "Shad."

My friend asked me who I was searching for and I told her the story. She agreed it would be nearly impossible to find a man whose face I couldn't recall. I didn't even pray that God would help me find him because I didn't really believe He would answer such a difficult prayer.

A FEW MINUTES before the service started, I happened to overhear a conversation behind me. The two men who were talking had never met, so they introduced themselves. One of them said, "Nice to meet you. My name is Shad—short for Shadrach."

No! Impossible! Right behind me?

I whirled around with tears in my eyes and reminded Shad how we had met at Christmas. He told me that my mother's prayers were being answered. I marveled at how God had put him right behind me in an audience of nearly 4,000 people and he said, "You know, I started to sit farther back, but I heard the Lord telling me to move up. And there was only one empty seat —right behind you."

I COULDN'T WAIT to call Mom and tell her the story. Finding Shad was indeed a miracle, but I believe the even bigger miracle was that God would orchestrate this impossible reunion just to encourage His faithful, sometimes discouraged, prayer warrior. He wanted to let Mom know in a personal, seemingly impossible way that He loved her and was listening to her every word when she prays. He truly did hear all of her prayers, even the unanswered ones.

THIS EASTER MIRACLE was meant for me, as well. I have no trouble believing in God's big miracles like the Christmas story and the empty tomb—I was praising Him that morning for the miracle of His resurrection from the dead. But for the small things in my life?

Surely God was too busy to micro-manage the little details. I have a few unanswered prayers of my own that I've been praying about for a long, long time. But when I consider the size of the crowd filling the auditorium—and overflowing into a second hall with a video screen—I can't deny that He performed a miracle that Resurrection Sunday. Only He could put the very stranger I was searching for in the seat right behind mine.

MY PRAYER TIME has been re-energized by my "chance" meeting with Shad. And I'll continue to pray for all of the impossible, unanswered needs on my list. Because the God who is listening is a God of small miracles as well as big ones.

Prayer

Heavenly Father, forgive me for forgetting that You are the God of the impossible. Thank You for all of the miracles You've done in our lives, the big ones and the small ones. When our prayers seem to go unanswered, help us to trust that Your miracle is waiting just around the corner.

FIFTY-ONE

COMPANIONS FOR THE JOURNEY

"If one falls down, his friend can help him up. But pity the man who falls and has no one to help him up! ... A cord of three strands is not quickly broken."

Ecclesiastes 10, 12

I'VE BEEN GOING through photographs from my bicycle trip through Europe last June, and before the memories fade, I want to share some lessons I learned along the way. My bike tour, like the Body of Christ, relied on three very important people—the Guide, the Corner, and the Sweep.

THE GUIDE, of course, is Jesus. He knows the way and all of the challenges we'll face. He has traveled this way before us. The Guide also knows the way to our final destination—the hotel—or to His Father's House in Heaven, where there's a place prepared for us. But we won't get there unless we follow Him.

Our Guide led us up some pretty steep paths, and through harrowing, traffic-congested cities. There were times I didn't want to follow him. But I knew that if I went my own way, I would get lost. Jesus said, *"I am the way . . . No one comes to the Father except through Me."*

THE CORNER CAN BE anyone in the group. When the Guide comes to an intersection with several choices, he turns to the rider behind him and says, "I need a Corner." The rider gets off his bike and waits at the intersection to point the way. When everyone has cycled past, the Corner rejoins the group. It's an important responsibility.

THE FIRST DAY of the trip, I didn't understand that there'd be a Corner to point the way, so I exhausted myself trying to keep the Guide in sight. And we can exhaust ourselves trying to follow Jesus, too. But He faithfully appoints members of His Body to serve as Corners at important crossroads, pointing the way.

We don't have to make this journey by ourselves. Jesus asks us to take our turn guiding others who are a little behind us on the journey. It means being ready, knowing scripture and the Guide's voice well enough to point the way.

On the second day of the trip, another newbie like me was told to be a Corner, and when she thought everyone had passed the intersection, she left her post. It turned out that 4 riders were still behind her, and they became lost. The Guide, like the Good Shepherd, left his flock to wait along the trail while he went back to "seek and save the lost."

. . .

THE SWEEP IS JUST as important as the Corner. Before setting out in the morning, the Guide asks for a volunteer to be the Sweep. The Sweep rides behind everyone else, waiting for stragglers and dawdlers and those who've grown weary.

Nobody enjoys being last, but a good Sweep cares about his slowpokes and waits patiently for them. When the Corner sees the Sweep, he knows that everyone has safely passed.

I THINK Jesus is pleased when we volunteer to be the Sweep and care for the stragglers. It's hard being patient with those who seem slow to learn, or who keep making the same mistakes in their journey. We can grow weary of sweeping up other people's messes. But a good Sweep shares the Shepherd's heart for the lost.

ONE DAY ON OUR TRIP, I was one of only three people in my group of 12 who was pedaling the old-fashioned way. The others rode e-bikes with batteries and 3-speed power-assist motors. I was feeling pretty proud of myself for tackling the journey on my own power—until we came to a very challenging hill. (We were in Switzerland, after all!)

I shifted into the lowest gears and gutted my way up the slope—still feeling proud. I was almost to the top—legs burning, lungs heaving—when I saw that the top wasn't the top! The road curved and the steep hill continued!

I was done. I had to get off and walk. The e-bikes zoomed past. Then the Sweep caught up with me. He also had an e-bike. I told him he could wait for me at the top, but he said, "No, I'm not leaving you behind."

He got off and walked beside me. After a minute or so he said, "Here, why don't you ride my bike and I'll ride yours?" I knew exactly how the man in Jesus' parable felt when he lay beaten along the road and the Good Samaritan loaned him his donkey! I swallowed the rest of my pride and accepted his offer. Zoom!—all the way to the top!

IT'S difficult to be the one who needs help. It's especially hard for me to confess that I'm weary and hurting and needing prayer. But the Guide has some very special people who have volunteered to be Sweeps.

They'll walk alongside us when the road becomes difficult —if we ask. And I also need to be willing to help someone else who has grown weary and walk with them along the way.

OUR JOURNEY OF DISCIPLESHIP, like my bike trip, is an exciting one. There are some amazing views at the top!

The best advice I can give, is to *"Trust in the Lord with all your heart and lean not on your own understanding; in all your ways acknowledge Him, and He will direct your path"* (Proverbs 3:6).

Have a great trip!

A FINAL WORD

Thank you for coming along on this journey with me as I've shared my stories. I hope you've been inspired and challenged by the many ways I've seen God working in my life. He's at work in all of our lives if we have eyes to see, teaching us about His love and helping our faith to grow.

Now that you've finished this book, I want to leave you with three exercises to try. These ideas have helped me grow closer to God over the years.

First, I keep a prayer journal to write down people and circumstances I'm praying for. The journal helps remind me of them when I sit down to pray during my quiet times. But I also leave space after each request to record how and when God answers those prayers. I'm always amazed to see how the things I prayed for were perfectly resolved in God's time and according to His plan. The journal serves as a reminder of His faithfulness, especially during the hard times when I don't even know how to pray.

Secondly, I recommend is that you take note of all the "God sightings" in your life. These are the moments and places where you saw God's hand, or little reminders of His love. It might be as simple as noticing His boundless creativity in the flowers in your garden. It could be a kind word someone offered just when you needed it. This book of devotionals describes some of the "God sightings" in my own life. Recording these little moments will provide you with an account of His goodness to remind you when He seems far away.

Finally, I encourage you to write down scripture verses that build your faith. Keep them in a handy place where you can read them regularly and commit them to memory. The Bible says, *"Your Word is a lamp to my feet and a light to my path"* (Psalm 119:105). It offers guidance and wisdom when we need it. Scripture is also part of every Christian's armor to battle the enemy. The Word of God is our "sword" (see Ephesians 6:10-18). We need to be well-armed.

And now that we've reached "The End," I would like to leave you with this blessing from God's Word:

"The Lord bless you and keep you; the Lord make His face shine upon you and be gracious to you; the Lord turn His face toward you and give you peace" (Numbers 6:25).

ABOUT THE AUTHOR

Lynn has sold more than one and a half million copies of her books worldwide. A former teacher who now writes and speaks full-time, she has won eight Christy Awards for her historical fiction. One of those novels, Hidden Places, has also been made into an Original Hallmark Channel movie. Lynn and her husband have raised three children and make their home in western Michigan. Learn more at www.lynnaustin.org

ALSO BY LYNN AUSTIN

Waves of Mercy

Legacy of Mercy

Where We Belong

Pilgrimage

All Things New

Wonderland Creek

While We're Far Apart

Though Waters Roar

Until We Reach Home

A Proper Pursuit

A Woman's Place

All She Ever Wanted

Hidden Places

Wings of Refuge

Eve's Daughters

Fly Away

Chronicles of the Kings Series

God And Kings

Song of Redemption

The Strength of His Hands

Faith of My Fathers

Among the Gods

———

CPSIA information can be obtained
at www.ICGtesting.com
Printed in the USA
FSHW012100141119
64124FS

9 780999 386316